A Common Place

A Common Place

The Representation of Paris in Spanish American Fiction

Julie Jones

Lewisburg
Bucknell University Press
London: Associated University Presses

Associated University Presses
440 Forsgate Drive
Cranbury, NJ 08512

Associated University Presses
16 Barter Street
London WC1A 2AH, England

Associated University Presses
P.O. Box 338, Port Credit
Mississauga, Ontario
Canada L5G 4L8

The paper used in this publication meets the requirements
of the American National Standard for Permanence of Paper
for Printed Library Materials Z39.48–1984.

Library of Congress Cataloging-in-Publication Data

Jones, Julie, 1943–
    A common place : the representation of Paris in Spanish American
fiction / Julie Jones.
        p.   cm.
    Includes bibliographical references (p.   ) and index.
    ISBN 0-8387-5378-7 (alk. paper)
    1. Spanish American fiction—20th century—History and criticism.
2. Paris (France)—In literature.   I. Title.
PQ7082.N7J63   1998
863—dc21   97-39915
                                                                    CIP

1001293160

Contents

Acknowledgments

Permission for *Distant Relations* (English translations of *Una familia lejana*): Excerpts from *Distant Relations* by Carlos Fuentes, translated by Margaret Sayers Peden. Translation copyright 1982 by Farrar, Straus & Giroux. Reprinted by permission of Farrar, Straus & Giroux.

Permission for *Distant Relations* for distribution in the U.K. and the Commonwealth, except Canada, granted by A. M. Heath: Copyright by Carlos Fuentes.

Permission for *Reasons of State* (English translation of *El recurso del método*): From *Reasons of State* by Alejo Carpentier. Copyright 1976 by Alfred A. Knopf Inc. Reprinted by permission of the publishers.

Permission for *Reasons of State* for distribution in the U.K. and the Commonwealth, except Canada, granted by A. M. Heath: Copyright by The estate of the late Alejo Carpentier.

An earlier version of chapter 2 of *A Common Place* was published under the same title in the *Revista Canadiense de Estudios Hispánicos*. Reprinted by permission from the *Revista Canadiense de Estudios Hispánicos* 15, no. 2 (1991).

An earlier version of chapter 4 was published under the title "Paris and 'el país' in 'El recurso del método'" in the *Romanic Review*. Reprinted by permission from the *Romanic Review* 83, no. 1 (1992). Copyright by the Trustees of Columbia University in the City of New York.

An earlier version of chapter 6 was published under the title "Text and Authority in Elena Garro's 'Reencuentro de personajes'" in the *Canadian Review of Comparative Literature*. Reprinted by permission from the *Canadian Review of Comparative Literature* 18, no. 1 (1991).

A Common Place

1

Antecedents and Patterns

ARRIVING IN PARIS IN 1891, PART OF THE FIRST BIG WAVE OF LATIN
Americans to land in the city, Enrique Gómez Carrillo is so disillusioned by his initial experience that he shuts himself up in
his room to reread Murger:

> To get away from the real world, I read *La Vie de Bohème* in search
> of the image that had filled my dreams. . . . More than once, during
> my first weeks in Paris, I preferred to spend the evening shut up in
> my room with those gallant spirits than to sit in the smoke-filled bar
> of the *pension*. (1974, 168)[1]

When Carrillo finally does open the door and venture out, it is
to impose his reading on what he finds there; Paris begins to
seem real to him only when it conforms to the expectations created by literature. The unmediated city is intractable, elusive,
and, therefore, unreal.

Scènes de la vie de Bohème (Henri Murger, 1845–59), the urban pastoral that seduced so many generations of artists, will
shape Carrillo's first experience of Paris. Once he has met Alice,
who will soon become his mistress, he is quick to recover from
his initial disillusionment with the city. Like Mimi Pinson, Alice
is "a Parisian and a dressmaker" (185). When she takes him to
the Polidor (which will later figure in Cortázar's 62), he is convinced he has entered

> a chapter out of Murger and that I was in the old Café Procope,
> paradise of hairy philosophers, or in the Cabaret Momus, where Col-
> line invited Schaunard to coffee. Without having tasted a drop of
> wine, I felt drunk, delirious, as though I had stepped out of time,
> out of life, into a kind of crazy paradise populated by charming
> ghosts. (186)

Surveying the clientele of the restaurant, he spots Rodolf, Marcel, Musette, and so on, and he concludes, inevitably, that Alice must be Mimi. Later he decides that he himself is not like a hero out of Murger only because he has money in his pockets.

This collation of what he sees with what he has read will determine all of the experience of Paris that Carrillo covers in the "En plena Bohemia" (In the middle of Bohemia) section of his autobiography. His description of life in Madrid, which follows hard on the heels of his first eight months in Paris, is very different. Even though he moves there at a point when he is still full of literary enthusiasm and meets the great writers of the time, the city seems immune to such treatment—at least to Carrillo; it is Alice who espouses the exotic view of Spain. But in Paris everything refers Carrillo back to art or literature. His friend Garay is like a character out of Bourget (184) or Hoffmann (212). The couples that go by recall Watteau (195). The seamstresses who labor in a nearby workshop are all like Mimi (196), and "in all the girls who wore silk skirts and fur-trimmed shawls, I saw heroines out of Henri Becque or Guy de Maupassant" (217), and to the girls in Bullier he attributes "very subtle psychological concerns" (218), much to their confusion. After all, he feels that he already knows both the women and the buildings, because "I had seen them in poems, in novels, in prints. . . . Were they not, in fact, my best friends?" (191). In the old part of the city, he expects to see chums of François Villon pop out at any moment, and later he convinces himself that he actually has seen Villon, wrapped in his cloak. In a moment of distress, he addresses the city in "the tone of Lamartine" (309), and when he and Alice are on the verge of leaving for Spain, he sees himself as Des Grieux and her as Manon Lescaut.

Alice, who introduces Carrillo to this *real* Paris, is herself infected by literature. After a long discourse on Bohemia, she comments with some embarrassment that if she seems pedantic it is because of the books she reads (188). Theirs is, then, a consciously cultivated way of seeing things. Carrillo tells how both of them make a point of studying the photographs of writers and artists exhibited in the window of the Pirou studio so that they can recognize those geniuses in the street:

it became a real obsession. On the streets, in the cafés, in the theaters, at any time, day or night, as soon as we spotted a face that was a little out of the ordinary, we began to find it an illustrious name. (272)

Clearly what matters here is not the reality that presents itself but the idea that orders it. In the same chapter, entitled with some irony "Glorious friends," Carrillo describes encounters with two of his idols, Banville and Leconte de Lisle. He carries on lengthy imaginary conversations with both men but astutely avoids actual contact. When he notices that Banville has become annoyed with the young man who follows him so pertinaciously, "afraid of hearing his irritated voice in reality, I drew away so that I could keep on listening to him . . . in my imagination" (269). And later, trailing Leconte de Lisle, he becomes so involved in their imaginary exchange that he loses sight of the man himself without realizing it. The poet and, in fact, the city itself are incidental to Carrillo's experience.

In "Ultima ilusión" (Last illusion), a story written at roughly the same time that Carrillo was finding his way in Paris, Julián del Casal presents a young Cuban who, like the author himself, has never been abroad. The character describes his reactions to the city in great detail. At the end of his peroration he decides, rather cannily, to skip the voyage. Only by staying at home, we infer, can he conserve his last illusion.

This fear that the thing itself might disappoint is hardly surprising, given the reputation that the city enjoyed at that time. Eighteen eighty-nine was the year of the World Exposition that produced the Eiffel Tower. It coincided with the opening of the Moulin Rouge and the installation of the first electric lights, which were to transform the city into La Ville Lumière. This modernization of the city also coincided with a period of very active territorial expansion that would convert France into a major colonial power and further increase the prestige of its capital and its culture.[2] At the same time, a corresponding economic expansion in the Americas allowed great numbers of Latin Americans (and North Americans as well) to take advantage of the attractions of Paris.

For the new middle classes, the trip to Paris became a way to emulate oligarchical practice; it was part of an ostentatious lifestyle that was derisively dubbed "rastaquouère" in a fanciful reference to leather-clad gauchos moving up the social and economic scale.[3] Equally anxious to find validation in Paris were the artists and intellectuals. Rubén Darío writes in his autobiography that even as a child he prayed every night for a chance to see Paris before he died (1950–55, 1:102), and in turn he, along with Amado Nervo, Manuel Gutiérrez Nájera, Carrillo, Casal, and scores of lesser writers, produced the chronicles, poems, and stories that helped consolidate the impression that Paris represented the summum bonum of human experience, "a paradise on earth where one could inhale the essence of happiness" (1950, my translation Darío 1:102).[4]

The difference in accent between this sort of exclamation and the letters in which Domingo Sarmiento describes his 1846 visit to Paris cannot be entirely ascribed to the brillance of Paris at the time. In fact, France had enjoyed considerable prestige in Latin America since the Enlightenment, and Sarmiento is full of admiration for the city, but he stops short of renouncing all other allegiances and instead makes note of the things he sees that might promote industry and civility at home (the cultivation of silk, the public dances, and the hippodrome).[5] By the 1880s, however, the situation of the intellectual in the greater Latin American capitals had changed. The rapid growth of the cities and the increasing insistence on professionalism meant that fewer writers would play substantial roles in their countries' political life. The press, catering to a growing readership, offered a livelihood, but little intellectual satisfaction or prestige. It was probably a combination of these factors—exclusion from public life at home, increased movement between the two continents, and a heightened perception of the city's glamour—that created among the artists and intellectuals what Sylvia Molloy calls "the thirst for exile that chose Paris as its destination" (my translation, 1972, 33).

By the turn of the century, then, Paris had been mythologized to such an extent among Spanish Americans—and, indeed, among people from all corners of the earth—that contact with the city itself had become problematic, at least for writers like Carrillo and Casal. A number of Spanish American novels of the period are set partially or entirely in Paris—Paul Groussac's *Fruto vedado* (1884), Eugenio Cambaceres's *Música sentimental*

(1884), Alberto del Solar's *Rastaquouère* (1890), Manuel Díaz Rodríguez's *Idolos rotos* (1901) and *Sangre patricia* (1902), Alberto Blest Gana's *Los trasplantados* (1904), and Ricardo Güiraldes's *Raucho* (1917). None of them, however, explores this problem, preferring to reproduce fairly standardized notions about the charms or the dangers of the metropolis without really questioning their models. Perhaps they were simply acceding to the demands of the marketplace. Carrillo himself wrote three novels that take place in Paris, all rather more decadent versions of *La vie de Bohème*—the best is perhaps *Maravillas, novela funambulesca* (1906). But in none of them does he treat this artistic background as a problem in itself. Only in the autobiography does he take as a theme the conjunction of his literary expectations with the actual city.

With the First World War, Latin American interest in Paris waned. In literature, the end of the war coincided with the beginning of *mundonovismo*, a turning toward the countryside for subject matter that produced *La vorágine* (1924), *Don Segundo Sombra* (1926) and *Doña Bárbara* (1929) and that lasted well into the thirties. Following generations continued to focus on the national, if not necessarily the rural, scene. Even Carpentier situates his earlier works entirely in America. From *Raucho* in 1917 to *Rayuela* in 1962, virtually no fictional works of any note take place in Paris (or, for that matter, in Europe). Among the exceptions are Joaquín Edwards Bello's *Criollos en París* (1933), Martín Aldao's *La vida falsa* (1943), and Sebastián Salazar Bondy's little volume of short stories, *Pobre gente de París* (1958).[6] As the title suggests, Aldao's novel is basically a reprise of the *exemplum vitandi* view of Paris. Salazar Bondy's and, especially, Edwards Bello's works reveal a more complex attitude toward the experience of Paris, but for them it is the city, rather than their representation of the city, that is problematic.

It is not until the nineteen sixties that Spanish American writers begin to confront openly and insistently the difficulties that accompany the desire to represent a place that has become a commonplace in art and literature. This development is part of the self-consciousness that characterizes postmodernism in general. It would have been impossible, however, had Spanish American fiction not matured to such an extent that writers felt they had earned artistic citizenship not only in Paris but, indeed, throughout the Western world, with all the rights this sense conferred—including license to make use of, without being subservient to, other literatures. According to Cortázar, it was around 1950 that Latin American writers began to free themselves from the dominant influence of French literature (1983, 202–3). *Into the Mainstream*, the English title of the book of interviews published by Barbara Dohmann and Luis Harss in 1966, signals the new position that Spanish American fiction would occupy in Western literature.

However, Paris itself continued to draw Spanish American writers, many of them refugees from the dictatorial regimes prevalent at the time, many attracted not only by the city but also by the presence of fellow Latin American intellectuals there. From the period following the Second World War until the early eighties when the democratic process had been firmly established in Spain, Paris was *the* gathering spot for Spanish American writers (Kohut, 1983, 16). When *Mundo Nuevo* was founded there in 1966, it was with the express intention of "bringing a Latin American accent to the truly international dialogue that has its center in Paris." The title refers to the "new world" of Latin American culture, "a culture without frontiers, free of dogma and fanatical servitudes" (my translation, "Presentación" 1966, 4).

The liberation from French literary tradition to which Cortázar refers and that is suggested in the presentation of *Mundo Nuevo* took many forms, as the novels that make up the Boom and the following period attest. But for writers wanting to deal with their experience of life in Paris, the play of text on text, the suggestion that perhaps there is no there there,[7] that Paris is a simulacrum, rather than a reality, provided both a strategy for dealing with the rather shopworn image of the city and an effort to establish their own literary claim to what has been called the "the secret literary capital of the Spanish-speaking world" (my translation, Kohut 1983, 16).

In discussing the way these texts insert themselves "into the mainstream"—that is, into modern metropolitan culture, whether that be seen as specifically French or not—I will refer often to parody. I am using the term in the acceptance Linda Hutcheon develops in her study of the subject—that is, as an *ironic inversion* of an earlier work, which may, but does not necessarily, include ridicule (1985, 6). Parody is simultaneously subversive of and complicit with the tradition in which it works, and it therefore is peculiarly well suited to convey the almost always ambivalent relation between the novelist from the periphery and the cultural center toward which that novelist gravitates. Parody, along with collage, another strategy frequent in these works, produces a hybrid text that in itself reproduces the ethnic and cultural mixture inevitable in this postcolonial world.

I have spoken of the works studied here as postmodern rather than postcolonial because all these novels are governed by concerns and strategies that position them within postmodernism and all of them are written from within the Western cultural tradition. Except for France's outrageous attempt to appropriate Mexico under Maximilian, an incident critical to *Una familia lejana*, the type of colonization at issue in the Spanish American republics in relation to France is cultural rather than political, and the writers involved are all of European descent (although Goytisolo, the only actual European in the group, has been described by Edward Said as having "crossed to the other [i.e., Arab] side," 1993, xx). Just what constitutes a postcolonial text is a somewhat vexed question (see, for example, During 1995; Appiah 1995; and Hutcheon 1995). All the novels studied here are clearly aware of the effects of cultural imperialism. Three of them—*Paisajes después de la batalla, Una familia lejana,* and *El recurso del método*—exhibit, in varying degrees, the overt political concern often considered essential to the postcolonial, but none of them falls within the field in sensu strictu. There is, however, a great deal of overlap between the postmodern, the postcolonial, and, for that matter, the feminist (Holst Petersen and Rutherford's *A Double Colonization,* 1996, explores this idea at length). The target of all three discourses—whether viewed primarily as humanism, imperialism, or patriarchy—is essentially the same, although the particulars may vary considerably, and the most frequently employed strategy is a counter-discourse that subverts the dominant discourse from within.

My study of the depiction of Paris in Spanish American fiction will focus, then, on the self-conscious incorporation of other texts as a means of exploring what Paris represents (in both senses of the word) for the writer, the protagonist, and the text that confront the city in its intractable reality. My focus is on novels written in and after the nineteen sixties, when writers begin systematically to articulate the literary problems involved in the encounter with the city. Although I make some reference to biography, I have chosen to concentrate primarily on the texts themselves,[8] and I have limited myself to one text per author in order to cover a broader spectrum. I have made a point of choosing works with markedly different approaches to my subject: Julio Cortázar's Rayuela (1963), Hopscotch [1966]); Julio Ramón Ribeyro's La juventud en la otra ribera (1969, Youth on the other bank of the river); Alejo Carpentier's El recurso del método (1974, Reasons of State [1976]); Carlos Fuentes's Una familia lejana (1980, Distant Relations [1982]); Elena Garro's Reencuentro de personajes (written in 1962, published in 1982, Reunion of characters); and, finally, a peninsular work closely related to the Spanish American perspective, Juan Goytisolo's Paisajes después de la batalla (1982, Landscapes after Battle [1987]).

Goytisolo's development of a multilayered, polymorphous, hallucinatory discourse aligns him to the most representative novels written in Spanish America during the period studied here. Fuentes includes him in La nueva novela hispanoamericana, and Goytisolo has explicitly aligned himself with the new Hispano-American narrative, which he describes as freer in relation to the past and in its use of other literatures than is peninsular fiction. It is perhaps fitting, then, that, although Goytisolo's parody is wide-ranging, the principal intertext of Paisajes, as I shall argue, is Rayuela, first term in this series of novels set in Paris. I have chosen to end my study with Paisajes because it self-consciously incorporates the discourse of Paris in its Spanish American configuration while at the same time showing substantial changes in the perception of Paris in the late twentieth century and in the function of Paris in late twentieth-century literature.

No matter what attitude the writer assumes toward Paris, the representation of the city in Spanish American letters involves a confluence of leitmotivs that persist, if often in ironic or parodic forms, throughout the self-conscious novel. Virtually all of them are present in Carrillo's work. I do not suggest that the repetition is conscious—it is not clear that these writers were familiar with Carrillo. But I simply suggest that the unusual development in Carrillo's autobiography of a highly self-conscious attitude toward the nature of the Paris experience for someone of a literary turn, in addition to the reliance on a number of *topoi* common to Spanish American writers in Paris, make his autobiography a very convenient starting point for this study. The running comparison that Carrillo so blithely sustains between what he has read about the city and what he sees or does within the city evolves into the trite romanticism that leads a middle-aged Peruvian administrator to his death at the hands of con artists in *La juventud en la otra ribera* and the nagging sense of inauthenticity that blights Horacio Oliveira's sojourn in the city in *Rayuela*.

The notion that his favorite literature has come to life around him and that he is part of that life helps convince the young Carrillo that he belongs. The autobiography serves the same function for the adult Carrillo. It is his version of Paris, and it is governed by the interplay between his younger self—the protagonist, who is just discovering the city—and his older self—the narrator, who proclaims that only in maturity has he really come to understand—in other words, possess—the city. Today this claim to possession conveyed by the urbane tone of the mature man about town that characterizes much earlier writing about the city sounds naive. Postmodern narrative records only the failure of that attempt, both in life and in literature. Yet this record constitutes the narrator's own territorial claim, if not to Paris itself, then to a portion of the representation of Paris.

Those representations repeat not only the resolute bookishness of Carrillo's autobiography, but other *topoi* present in Carrillo as well, *topoi* that are common to much fin-de-siècle writing about Paris. For Carrillo, as for other *modernistas*, the "real" Paris is not the monumental city, which leaves him cold, but the sexualized city:

> a frivolous, voluptuous, frou-frou Paris, smelling of rice powder . . . with its eyelids a bit blue from the bad nights, with small and exquisite graces, with an air of sensuality that made me feel drunk immediately. (1974, 170)

Not coincidentally he meets Alice, who works as a milliner at the Louvre department store, and he discovers the "real" Paris at the same time.

The motif of the grisette-guide, who will introduce the protagonist to the essential Paris appears in a number of early works and resurfaces years later in *La juventud en la otra ribera* and in *Rayuela* (in the latter by way of André Breton's *Nadja*, as I will argue in chapter 2). In this schema, the woman and the city are conflated; possession of the one signals possession of the other; further, the "real" city is seen in terms of the working-class quarters associated with the woman. This metonymic process is by no means limited to Spanish American letters. Nadja revealed a new Paris to Breton; Maurice Chevalier sang of the city as if it were a woman; and much of the popularity of *chanteuses* like Yvette Guilbert, Lucienne Boyer, and Edith Piaf lay in the carefully fostered notion that they embodied the essential (i.e., popular) Paris.[9] Yet the idea that by conquering the right woman one may conquer the city as well must be peculiarly attractive to the outsider. It is, in fact, a motif found in much travel literature, as Eric J. Leed points out in *The Mind of the Traveler*: "Historically, men have traveled and women have not . . . an arrangement that has defined the sexual relations in arrivals as the absorption of the stranger—often young, often male—within a nativizing female ground" (1991, 112).

And, as I have suggested, many of these novels are concerned with the acquisition of Paris—if only in the imagination. An illustrative early text that addresses this subject is a little story by Gutiérrez Nájera: "Stora y las medias parisienses" (Stora and the Parisian stockings). The hero is a poor poet whose name suggests that he is a foreigner. This poet is prey to an obsession. On rainy days, when the Parisiennes must raise their skirts to avoid the mud, thus showing off a bit of calf, Stora devotes himself to following, not so much the women, as their footwear:

> with his eye fixed on their shoes and stockings, he would follow them night and day, walking and walking like a Wandering Jew; he would see the squares and the streets disappear, would leave the boulevards behind to lose himself in the darkest and muddiest quarters, giving up a blue stocking for a grey one, or a little black kid boot for a flashy gold slipper. (My translation, 1958, 83)

One day he wins a small fortune and retires to the Mediterranean to try to cure the chest infection brought on by his former poverty and his obsession, but away from Paris he pines. Finally, he returns to the city and to his old habit, catches a cold, and dies. Gutiérrez Nájera describes his demise as a kind of triumph:

> Poor Stora! What prince, what millionaire, what nabob, has satisfied his caprices as well? In his imagination, Paris belonged to Stora; it had been conquered by his invincible desire. (84)

The woman, then, is a vehicle that affords the protagonist a certain angle of vision, but inevitably his are the eyes that see, and his is the imagination that captures Paris. Reduced to their footwear, Stora's women are an emanation of the passing scene, and *that* is the real object of Stora's desire.

In some novels the woman is not present at all, but the search for, or claim to, inside knowledge, a certain vision of the "real" Paris, on the part of the protagonist, is almost standard issue even in the self-conscious novels that assert the instability or irreality of the "real"; indeed, it is voiced as far back as Sarmiento. Jonathan Culler argues that this idea of seeing the inside of things is a "powerful touristic topos, essential to the structure of tourism" (1982, 131).[10] The young Carrillo, Horacio Oliveira, and the protagonist of *La juventud en la otra ribera* depend on the help of a woman (as, too, do the protagonists of Edwards Bello's *Criollos en París* and Salazar Bondy's *Pobre gente de París*). The older Carrillo claims to have achieved it in his maturity by dint of much experience. The Head of State of *El recurso del método* tries to achieve it through his discriminating taste as well as his penchant for slumming—for him it is simply *savoir vivre*. The Fuentes character in *Una familia lejana* is forced into it by his friend Branly—the knowledge is both a revelation and a curse. And the narrator-protagonist of *Paisajes* finds it, paradoxically, in that third-world enclave, the Sentier.

In any event, this idea of possessing Paris—whether through access to a woman, by pounding the pavement alone, or by some other means—is a peculiarly masculine concept. The freedom that was so lauded by outsiders—Cortázar comments that Latin Americans traditionally thought coming to Paris, "in personal terms, offered absolute freedom" (my translation, 1983, 202)— turns on the ability to roam the city at will, a privilege that until recently was not vouchsafed a woman alone and even now leaves her vulnerable to assault. The *flâneur* is always a man; the "art of slumming," as Adrien Rifkin calls it, is a partriarchal practice (1993, 9). In the novels where a woman guides the protagonist through the maze of Paris, it is suggested that she can do so because intuitively and metonymically she embodies the city; she cannot *see* the city because she *is* the city.[11]

All this may explain why Garro's *Reencuentro de personajes* takes such a different attitude toward Paris. Here the protagonist, Verónica, is a victim both of the city and of the abusive lover who abandons her there. While Paris offers him an opportunity to realize his sexual fantasies and his projects for advancement, for Verónica it simply spells loss: of home, of security, of identity. She is there because of Frank, not through her own designs. For expatriate women in her situation—that is, women attached to a dominant partner—Shari Benstock points out,

> the Paris community did not provide the occasion to rewrite the paternalistic law but offered a further reinforcement of it, the more painful because masked by many illusory freedoms, the most seductive (and destructive) of which was the freedom to explore erotic and emotional relationships outside the bounds of marriage. (1986, 452)

Dependent on the whims of others, convinced that her life has already been decided, Verónica sees Paris as *unheimlich*; in all its expanse, she can find no little corner to curl up in. Far from possessing the city, she loses possession even of herself there.

The question of identity in relation to the experience of Paris is critical. In his study of the careers of North American writers resident in Paris during the modernist period, J. Gerald Kennedy argues that Paris offered each of them "a complex image of the possibilities of metamorphosis" (1993, xiii). My concern here is not primarily biographical, but a number of these works flaunt the overlap between biography and fiction, and all of them revolve around the notion of transformation effected in, and often by, Paris, whether this be seen in artistic, personal, or social terms, and whether it be achieved or denied. A number of earlier works—among them *Los trasplantados*, *Rastaquouère*, and *La vida falsa*—were much concerned about the new classes' attempt to use the city for social advancement. This intent is satirized in *El recurso del método*, where the low-born dictator moves to Paris in order to acquire *bon ton* and, as he puts it, become a person (1976, 303; 1974a, 334). It is also satirized in *Una familia lejana*, where the Fuentes character has become so elegant and so French that he feels offended when someone reminds him of his origin. More typically, however, the Spanish American novel that includes a sojourn in Paris turns on the possibilities for metamorphosis adumbrated in Carrillo's autobiography. That is, personal (often sexual) and artistic realization, is seen more often than not—certainly this is the case with Carrillo—as one and the same. This is the tantalizing possibility that the city holds out to Horacio Oliveira, to Ribeyro's protagonist (who feels his life has become as exciting as a novel), and even to Goytisolo's narrator-protagonist, who develops his identity as an underground man within the confines of the Sentier. Finally, it is in Paris that Carpentier's Head of State, now an Ex, reassumes his primitive identity through a process of entropy. And it is also in Paris that the Fuentes character is forced to recognize, even embrace, the origin he sought, rather foolishly, to elide; it is with pride as well as fear that he becomes aware of the ghostly Spanish American presence there.

Except for *Paisajes*, all these novels depend, whether implicitly or explicitly, on the opposition between Paris and Latin America. Sometimes it is simply a hint of what the protagonist has escaped from—in *La juventud* Peru is reduced to Huamán's thin wife and thirty years of working in the bureaucracy—or would escape to—in *Reencuentro* it is the authentic, paternal home that would save Verónica from the frightening reinactment of prior narrations. For Horacio Oliveira, who "reads" Paris as a sum of reified texts representing Western civilization, Buenos Aires has not yet been written. Yet curiously, this makes it less rather than more "real" than Paris, and his adventures there have an oddly abstract quality—perhaps because it was so familiar to Cortázar that it had become invisible.

It is in Carpentier's and Fuentes's novels that the relationship between France and Latin America is most thoroughly explored. Both writers emphasize the interpenetration of the two cultures. Although Carpentier is concerned with the effect of French culture on Latin America, the novel ends with the establishment of a kind of Caribbean beachhead in the attic of the ex-president's elegant mansion on the rue de Tilsitt. This ending looks forward to and in some ways inspires—Fuentes refers to it specifically in an interview—*Una familia lejana.* Fuentes focuses on the incursion of Latin America in Paris in the form of writers working in both French and Spanish—that is, on the image of Paris as the literary capital of Spanish America. But he also identifies the Latin American element with the image of a jungle lurking in the heart of Paris. Latin America, then, also stands, in psychic terms, for a side of French life that is widely denied.

For Goytisolo, the poor Arab immigrants of the Sentier stand for that side of life while Spain in general and Barcelona in particular share the social and intellectual repressiveness and the consumerism that he denounces in bourgeois Paris and the rest of Europe. For Goytisolo, then, to invert the cliché, Europe does *not* end at the Pyrenees. If Fuentes imagines Paris as invaded by Latin America, Goytisolo envisages it, quite happily, as overrun by Africa and the Middle East.

So, whether it is loved or hated, the city persists as an icon, at least for this generation of writers. But it is a very different city now from the one Carrillo praised and even from the one Cortázar knew. As Jerrold Seigel points out, "tensions between Bohemia and the rest of society have diminished . . . permitting the migration of once Bohemian practices toward the center of social life" (397). Paris, then, is no longer vital to an experience of artistic and personal freedom. Nor is it the essential meeting point for Spanish American artists and intellectuals that it was through the greater part of this century. With the consolidation of democracy in Spain, the literary capital of the Spanish-speaking world has now moved to Barcelona. If Paris still commands the respect of younger writers, this is due primarily to its glorious past, a past that includes the novels to be examined in this study.

2

The City as Text:
Reading Paris in *Rayuela*

What I always find here in Paris is the mental stimulus that comes from just walking down a street and seeing how this city works.
                                        —Cortázar (my translation, 1983)

RAYUELA (HOPSCOTCH),[1] A NOVEL INSCRIBED AGAINST WESTERN SOCI-ety, thought, and art, takes place in Paris—stronghold of that civilization—for more than half of its pages. Julio Cortázar treats the city as a palimpsest and Oliveira's experience as a "reading" of prior texts. This strategy enables him to subvert the clichés so often associated with the Latin American view of Paris by encompassing them in his own work, and it provides a target for his criticism of a logocentric discourse. Cortázar does not extend this treatment to Buenos Aires, second locus of the novel, be-cause, like other far-flung capitals, it is eccentric in terms of Western civilization. There is no suggestion that Oliveira at-tempts to "read" Buenos Aires in the way he tries to "read" Paris. Buenos Aires does not serve as an intertext in the novel; Paris does. To convey this idea of Paris, Cortázar refers the reader either to earlier works—the love story, for example, is an ex-tended parody of Breton's *Nadja*—or to language itself. Paris, we are told, "is one big metaphor" (1966, 132; 1987, 159), but it is a metaphor without a fixed referent. The Paris that confronts the reader of *Rayuela* is exposed as a verbal construct. Yet, curiously, at the same time as he insists that reality can never be experi-enced except at a remove, Cortázar voices repeatedly the longing for full possession, for original experience. This combination of derision and wishful thinking that informs the parody of *Nadja* sets the tone most characteristic of *Rayuela*. In the following pages, I shall examine in detail Cortázar's development of Paris as an intertext and the tension resulting from his paradoxical desire to escape literature.

The first section of *Rayuela* is riddled with other texts; they enter the novel through reference, allusion, quotation, and discussion. Cortázar has commented that in this book "I am somehow paying my debts [to French literature]" (my translation, 1983, 211), but perhaps the word "somehow" should be stressed. Frequently these evocations of earlier works are parodic, and parody, as Linda Hutcheon points out, cuts both ways (1985, 37). It can judge the target text by the standard of the contemporary or the contemporary by the standard of the target text (57). In *Rayuela* it does both. Parody is, of course, part of Cortázar's meditation on fiction and part of his argument in favor of a new kind of book, but it also suggests the difficulty of transcending established modes of being—especially in Paris, where every experience seems to have been already written. The use to which he puts Benito Pérez Galdós's *Lo prohibido*, interpolated derisively in chapter 34, illustrates the movement of irony in these allusions. Oliveira's running commentary on the novel, interspersed between the lines of Galdós's text, deflates the smug tone of the earlier work and exposes what appears to be a solid bourgeois world as a verbal construct by forcing the reader to pay attention to the physical form of the *printed* page. It takes literally the expression "to read between the lines." But the lengthy quotation from the earlier work also reminds the reader that this story of a young man who comes from the provinces to try his fortune in the capital, whether Madrid or Paris, is the story of the present protagonist.

Oliveira is a kind of anti-Quixote (and for this reason in many ways like Quixote): a reader-hero who, in his effort to circumvent the received ideas of Western civilization, has set himself the mandate of *not* living according to literature.[2] He fails, of course. Reality, as Horacio perceives it, and as it reaches the reader through the medium of the text, is unavoidably bookish. Perico Romero accuses him of having come to Paris, like all Latin Americans, "to get their 'sentimental education'" (52; 69), a contention underlined by the citation from *Música sentimental* (itself inspired by Flaubert's *L'Education sentimental*) in chapter

153. Berthe Trépat sees in his situation a reflection of her own life conceived in terms of a feuilleton:

> What he was looking for was—
> "Beauty, exaltation, the golden bough," Berthe Trépat said. "Don't say a word, I can make a perfect guess. I also came to Paris, from Pau, quite a few years ago, looking for the golden bough." (114; 139)

His rejection of those things dear to the nineteenth-century novel—common decency, home, family—leads Oliveira to abandon the security of Buenos Aires and to take up life on the Left Bank. But this move simply involves substituting one genre for another: "the choice of what could be called nonconduct rather than conduct . . . faddish indecency instead of social decency" (12; 25). The long set piece describing the Club's meeting recalls the writing of the Beats—Oliveira classifies the party scene, with its atmosphere of smoke and liquor and jazz, as "literature, after all" (75; 94). These "normal bohemians" (13; 26), living a "pseudo-student existence" (3; 15), also recall, albeit with a change in key, the *modernista* cenacle of disinterested young artists (Horacio is identified mockingly with the hero of Darío's "El pájaro azul" [The blue bird], 23; 39), which in turn looked back with marked nostalgia to Murger's cheerfully unselfconscious dabblers (La Maga's real name is Lucía, "like Mimi in *La Bohème*," 43; 59). The artist's experience is no more authentic than the tourist's; it is, in fact, another guise of tourism. *La vie de bohème* is reduced to "a postcard with a drawing by Klee next to a dirty mirror" (11; 24).

If *Scènes de la vie de bohème* is for the Spanish American modernists the standard by which their experience of Paris is to be measured, for Cortázar the Golden Age of the city is the early twentieth-century period of artistic experimentation, which culminated in surrealism. Jean Franco points out that the novel focuses not on the urban experience itself but on "a literary vision of the city filtered through the Surrealists" (my translation, 1976, 276). Surrounded by students reading Durrell and Beauvoir, Horacio sees himself as

> already beyond the adolescent vogue, the cool, with an *Etes-vous fous?* of René Crevel anachronistically in my hands, with the whole

body of surrealism in my memory, with the mark of Antonin Artaud in my pelvis, with the Ionisations of Edgard Varèse in my ears, with Picasso in my eyes. . . . (92; 112)

Though a number of works figure here, the dominant intertext is Breton's *Nadja*. La Maga and the "fabulous Paris" (21; 36) to which she introduces Horacio are clearly intended as tongue-in-cheek imitations of *Nadja* and the view of Paris Breton elaborates in his narration. The parody here is more playful than belittling; if anything, it tends to turn against Oliveira, and, although it may have fun at the expense of Breton's book, there is an element of wishful thinking in this rendition of a more optimistic narration.[3]

First, as the names suggest, La Maga (The Magician), that highly literary representation of spontaneity, is modeled fairly closely on Nadja, who was actually a real woman. Elsewhere Breton describes the surrealist heroine as a magician (Cardinal 1986, 41). Both women come from outside Paris and from poor backgrounds. Both have had various lovers, and each has an illegitimate child who lives in the country and whom she adores. Nadja sometimes has her hair done so as to imitate Melusina or dresses to imitate Madame de la Chevreuse; La Maga tries to copy the hairdo of Eleanor of Aquitaine. Both are known by nicknames. Each disappears mysteriously from the work—Nadja into a mental asylum, La Maga either to parts unknown or into the Seine (Nadja, too, speaks of the possibility of suicide).

Curiously, although both books affirm a belief in regenerative love as a way out of emotional impasse, both protagonists refuse that love when it is offered (in a *coda* Breton claims to have found it with "X"). Oliveira deserts La Maga, realizing only later that he loves her. Breton, frustrated because Nadja does not always live up to his ideal ("a true conception of her worth," 1960, 135), abandons her to what he realizes will be an unhappy fate. His comment, "perhaps I have not been adequate to what she offered me" (135), serves either case. In the final analysis, both women provide a means to a different dimension of life, reached through intuition, not through intellect. Breton writes that reality is "lying at Nadja's feet like a lapdog" (111) and that

I have seen her fern-colored eyes open mornings on a world where the beating of hope's great wings is scarcely distinct from the other sounds which are those of terror and, upon such a world, I had as yet seen eyes do nothing but close. (111)

In a similar vein, Cortázar tells us that "La Maga was always reaching those great timeless plateaus that they were all seeking through dialectics" (25; 41). The two figures serve primarily as intercessors (La Maga is associated persistently with bridges) who put the protagonists in touch with an intensified reality.

The similarities between these two heroines are inseparable from the authors' conceptions of Paris. For both women, the zone of illumination is coextensive with the streets of the city, "the only region of valid experience" (Breton, 1966, 113). The street provides opportunity and freedom; it is here that both pairs of lovers meet for the first time and that they continue to meet by preference. For their lovemaking, Oliveira and La Maga opt for exploring that extension of the street, the hotel room, that allows them to penetrate—I use the term advisedly—different arrondissements.[4] Breton and Nadja, Oliveira and La Maga meet without setting up meetings in series of encounters that defy all probability (Breton 1966, 77, 91; Cortázar 1966, 3, 31–32, and 87–88; 1987, 15, 46–47 and 107–8). These meetings seem to prove the existence of objective chance, union of necessity and desire.

The activity and the concentration of people characteristic of major cities produce the bizarre coincidences that may be understood as signals; hence the importance of knowing how to interpret the city. Convinced that there is a secret tunnel extending from the Palais de Justice and circling the Hôtel Henri IV, Nadja intuits hidden connections, and La Maga shows Horacio what to look for in the streets and behind the doorways:

> she was already giving him lessons in how to look at and see things; lessons she was not aware of, just her way of stopping suddenly in the street to peep into an entranceway where there was nothing, but where a green glow could be seen further in. . . . (22; 37)

In this view, elaborated in both novels, Paris is a cryptogram in which the crisscross streets, the alleyways, the shop fronts, the store windows, the signs, the passersby all hold the potential for revelation, a revelation that may be facilitated by the presence of a certain kind of woman.

The parallels between the two novels are striking, but *Rayuela* is not simply an imitation of *Nadja*; it diverges in ways that are important. It is, to use a phrase Hutcheon takes from John Fowles, "both a homage and a kind of thumbed nose" (1985, 33) to the older text. Cortázar seems to be particularly amused at Breton's tendency to take himself very seriously—a tendency reflected in his descriptions both of Nadja and of the episodes he regards as signficant.

For one thing, Breton indicates only obliquely that his relationship with Nadja involves sex. She is important to him solely as intercessor. As Walter Benjamin points out, what matters in the book is not sensual pleasure but illumination (1978, 181). However, the implication that Breton and Nadja are largely indifferent to physical concerns gets short shrift in *Rayuela*. Cortázar is quick to expose the sexual underpinnings of intercession although he does not thereby denigrate La Maga's role. For Oliveira, as for Cortázar, sex is an essential part of any attempt to reach full presence. Nadja's description of herself as "the soul in limbo" (71) could hardly be applied to La Maga, intuitive but never fey, possessed of a brusque common sense and a fondness for oysters. It is not, perhaps, very surprising that Breton, who begins with a real woman, should mythicize—almost to the point of dehumanizing—her, whereas Cortázar, whose point of departure is literature, should take pains to make La Maga believably human.

The high seriousness with which Breton treats Nadja extends to much of the narration. In fact, a number of the "petrifying coincidences" (19) that suggest to Breton the imminence of some sort of revelation are striking primarily because of the contrast between the apparently trivial nature of the occurrence and the solemnity of the account (for a case in point, see 27–28). Cortázar deflates the portentousness of this kind of incident by exposing its ludicrous (and ludic) side. Humor, missing in *Nadja*, is important in *Rayuela*. In a list of "quietly exceptional things" (8; 20–21), for example, Oliveira includes the following:

going into a *pissotière* on the Rue de Médicis and seeing a man apply himself to his urination and then step back from the urinal towards me as he holds in the palm of his hand as if it were a precious and liturgical object a member of incredible colors and dimensions, and

my realizing at that moment that this man is the replica of another
. . . who twenty-four hours before in the Salle de Géographie had
been lecturing on totems and taboos and had held up carefully in
the palm of his hand ivory sticks. . . . (8; 21)

His description of La Maga, whom he imagines combing the
street for a piece of red cloth, convinced that something terrible
will happen if she does not find it (8; 21), and the involved and
absurd relation of his attempt to locate a sugar cube that has
rolled under the table at a posh restaurant (9–10; 22–23) have
the same effect: to assert the existence of uncanny episodes while
simultaneously questioning their value. The humor makes for a
livelier narration, but it undermines belief.

This last point brings us to the difficulty Cortázar has in *Ray-*
uela of affirming anything but need. He seems to regard the alternative reality that Breton posits in *Nadja* as essential but
unlikely. Breton's Paris, in a parodic version, becomes a kind of
absurd utopia viewed with a mixture of skepticism and longing,
never quite affirmed, never quite dismissed. The novel moves in
a pendular motion between the "unless . . ." (itself lifted from
Nadja, Breton 1960, 91) with which Oliveira suggests a gap in
reality that would open the way to authentic existence and an
attitude best summed up in Jake Barnes's words: "Isn't it pretty
to think so?" (Hemingway 1954, 247). Cortázar's extensive use
of parody simply reinforces the "unbearable ambiguity" (535;
604) that characterizes the entire novel.[5]

Parody, then, subverts not only one text in relation to another
but also the parodic text in relation to reality. This anti–
illusionist stance is part of Cortázar's attack on the realist novel,
which he sees as disingenuous. Since the ideal of full presence
is impossible to achieve in writing, it is best perhaps to be honest
about that fact by reminding the reader that what is imitated
here is literature and not life. A related strategy is to reduce
description to linguistic signifiers in an effort to approximate
original innocence. Morelli, in his search for authenticity, would
strip literature down to its elements (429; 488). He is particularly
attracted to the art of the Middle Ages "where everything has
value as a sign and not as a theme of description" (480; 545).

In *Rayuela*, Paris is conveyed primarily through the use of
street names, which proliferate, forming a nexus of itineraries

we can follow in an atlas; that is, the city is presented as map
rather than scene. Occasionally, there is a reference to a bridge,
a doorway, pavement: the city's most basic elements. The insistence on the detail instead of the whole has the same effect as
the insistence on the street name; it renders the city abstract.
Names, stones: the two are brought together in Morelli's repro-
duction of the tablets of Ur, the earliest known example of writing. Like the tablets, Paris is a primitive text, a series of signs
that readers must decipher or even invent meanings for, instead
of an alternative reality that we need only enter. According to
Oliveira, "any street corner of any city was the perfect illustra-
tion of what he had been thinking" (100; 122). Even the florid
passages that Cortázar calls "watercolors" of the city (1985, 110;
see, for example, chapter 73) are concerned with the movement
of language, not the representation of a world. The repeated attempts to define Paris in metaphoric terms are part of the same
tendency to reduce the city to language. Paris is a "ball of yarn"
(13; 26), "the Great Screw" (384–85; 440); "the shadow of a dove
[that] rubs up against the excrement a dog has left behind" (476;
540); "one fucking staircase after another" (433; 492); "a postcard
with a drawing by Klee next to a dirty mirror" (11; 24); "a center
. . . a mandala . . . a labyrinth" (427; 485); "a great blind love"
(135; 163); "the gates of assorted hells" (179; 214). In short,
"Paris is one big metaphor" (132; 159, 133; 161 and 180; 215),
and, as we shall see later, the explanation that Gregorovius gives
for this contention returns us once again to the realm of language.

Walter Benjamin writes that "the reader, the thinker, the loi-
terer, the flâneur are types of illuminati" (1978, 190). To study
the city as a text is to be alert to its signs; Oliveira "guesses that
in some part of Paris, some day or some death or some meeting
will show him a key; he's searching for it like a madman" (133;
160), hence the repeated references to postcard reproductions of
Klee. The key would confer "the freedom of the city" (180; 215):
understanding and presence.[6] Yet the key that is finally vouchsafed to Oliveira—the key to Morelli's flat, which provides access
to Morelli's files—offers understanding through literature; it is
the key to a code. In any event, it comes to Horacio too late—he
turns it over to Etienne "as if he were surrendering a city" (558;
629).[7] Still, the fact that the old man whose bedside he visits
in an uncharacteristically kind gesture should turn out quite

unexpectedly to be the Club's idol and that his flat should lie practically next door to the Club headquarters does suggest the possibility of a coherent reading of the city.

Morelli's comments, written on scraps of paper filed away in the apartment, indicate that to read the city, which is also, of course, the world, is to write it. On one scrap, he has noted: "the world is a figure, it has to be read. By read let us understand generated" (379; 435); and again, "writing is sketching my mandala and at the same time going through it" (402; 458). (Oliveira calls Paris "a mandala through which one must pass without dialectics," 427; 485.) Cortázar has pointed out that he wrote the Paris scenes of the novel on scraps of paper in cafés all over the city (1985, 110). The café, meeting place of the inner and outer worlds, is an ideal vantage point for the writer/flaneur to observe what the street brings. Hopscotch, of course, is *always* inscribed on the pavement, and it is the streets and sidewalks that furnish Oliveira with the objets trouvés from which he fashions his sculptures, works as open as the novel. The ideal city, a state of mind that is the goal of Cortázar's utopian aspirations, is not Paris, but it is linked to Paris—specifically to the Parisian streets—and not, for example, to Buenos Aires. Both heavenly city and earthly city are united in the figure of La Maga, who is related to Babylon through references (11 and 427–28; 24 and 486) suggesting that the sensual life must be an essential part of the new Jerusalem.[8]

For Cortázar, the woman is not only a guide to Paris and its hidden possibilities, she *is* the city; to possess her is to conquer the city (and what are the definitions of Paris, its reduction to language, other than attempts to possess it?). In Latin American writing that involves Paris, the hero's relationship with a grisette modeled on Mimi in *Scènes de la vie de bohème*—that is, a woman familiar with the streets of Paris—came to represent his dominion of the foreign capital. La Maga, who lives in the Hôtel de Paris, tempts Oliveira with "that *bohemia* of body and soul" (italics mine, 96; 116) that he longs to enter. The "Maga world" (6; 18) is coextensive with the "fabulous Paris" (21; 36) to which she introduces Horacio. Later, disillusioned with the potential of Paris and La Maga for changing his life, Oliveira continues to associate the two: "I held out my hand and touched the tangled ball of yarn which is Paris, its infinite material all wrapped up around itself" (13; 26). The physical gesture, the proximity of La Maga next to him in bed, the words *ball of yarn* and *wrapped around*: all suggest the connection. After he has left La Maga, Oliveira reflects that "it's as though I weren't in Paris" (corrected translation, 115; 140).

The woman-city equation is true not only of La Maga. Pola is "Pola Paris"; her body seen against the window of the apartment becomes the skyline of the city:

> pole of Paris, Paris of Pola, the greenish light of a neon sign going on and off against the yellow raffia curtain, Pola Paris, Pola Paris, the naked city with its sex in tune to the palpitation of the curtain. Pola Paris, Pola Paris, *every time more his.* . . . (my italics, 424; 481–82)

Pola is connected with the streets through the sidewalk drawings that she admires. Horacio asks rudely, "Are you made of chalk too?" (366; 421), and he imagines her being obliterated by the street cleaners and re-created the following day by the sidewalk artists. But, as Steven Boldy points out, with her collection of stylish books, her modish interest in Latin American folk culture, and her ample income, she also represents the liberal bourgeois experience of Paris (1980, 116). Her neat, attractive apartment stands in sharp contrast to the Bohemian quarters that La Maga inhabits. Stricken with cancer, she is part of a diseased social order that, like the chalk drawings, appears fragile but is paradoxically resistant to change.

La Maga is linked both to Pola (see especially 138; 166) and, more emphatically, to the *clocharde*, Emmanuèle, of whom she says, "I'm like her" (466; 530). She discerns a certain symmetry between Emmanuèle's relationship with the indifferent Celestin and her own with Horacio. There are other parallels: both women are blonde, Emmanuèle drapes herself in pieces of red cloth, and Oliveira imagines La Maga searching for a bit of red cloth.[9] Both sing *Les Amants du Havre*, both arrived by boat (La Maga from Montevideo, Emmanuèle from downriver), and both are associated with the Seine. Pola and Emmanuèle are also connected; when the *clocharde* is making love to him, Horacio puts his hand on her hair and thinks for a moment "that it was Pola's hair, that still once more Pola had thrown herself on top of him" (212;

250). Incarnation of *les bas fonds*, Emmanuèle lives on the street, sleeps by the Seine, and makes love to Oliveira on the sidewalk. She introduces him to the underworld, region of crime and destitution, a necessary corollary of Pola's Paris.

Significantly, Oliveira meets all of these women in the street. Berthe Trépat is another of his "found objects," encountered in a concert hall where he seeks refuge from the rain, and whose name sounds suspiciously like "trépas" (death). They provide him entrée to the Paris of the artist, the Bohemian, the middle class, and the impoverished. Emmanuèle's name hints that salvation may come to Oliveira through his nightmare experience of the underworld, a kind of transcendence downward that also involves knowing—in both senses of the word—the city *au fond*, or it may simply be an ironic commentary on his failure to do so. The novel remains ambiguous.

The woman, then, is both the city and the guide to the city; she is the thing itself and outside the thing. The apparent contradiction is subsumed in *Rayuela*, which is simultaneously novel and commentary. Oliveira is "the accomplice-reader"—as opposed to the "female-reader" (398; 454). I suspect that Cortázar used his two terms with greater intent than he would later admit to. Oliveira allows the woman to guide him as he reads the city-text through her body. Emmanuèle, who dresses in layers of clothing garnered from the city rubbish and sleeps wrapped in pages of *France Soir*, is a human palimpsest.

Gregorovius explains his contention that Paris is a metaphor by means of a parable about the tapestry on which he allegedly played as a child, a tapestry that depicts a map of the legendary city of Ophir with, at its center, the quarters of the Queen of Sheba. In this tapestry, the city is seen as a map (i.e., a text) and as a woman. The baby Ossip, in a movement analogous to hopscotch, storms the city and gains entrance to the quarters of Sheba. What the child reaches through innocence the artist does through experience. By means of his art, the creator of the tapestry also takes possession of that fabulous kingdom.

To Oliveira, with his bad French and his memories of Buenos Aires, and quite possibly to the young Cortázar as well, the real Paris remains huge and inhospitable. The theme of disenfranchisement is sounded again and again in the novel. However, seen as a woman or as a text, the city becomes more manageable.

Franco argues that "'Paris' is a city, but not *the* city in Cortázar's work" (my translation, 1976, 271). Yet perhaps the persistent search for the heavenly city that takes place in Paris is, as much as a desire for the utopian ideal, a displaced effort to possess that earthly city in its teeming reality. *Rayuela* turns on the impossibility of that quest. By drawing attention to the literary and linguistic nature of the city he has created here, Cortázar acknowledges openly, if ruefully, that the "real" Paris must always remain alien to the realm of fiction. It is only as a structure of words, a verbal tapestry, that the writer can ever possess Paris.

3
Dreams of a Golden Age:
La juventud en la otra ribera

IN JULIO RAMÓN RIBEYRO'S *LA JUVENTUD EN LA OTRA RIBERA* (YOUTH
on the other bank of the river),[1] images of Paris in earlier periods
and the accompanying ethos are projected against the mid-twen-
tieth-century city. The novella simultaneously parodies the notion of a golden age of belief and suggests the romantic necessity
of such an ideal. Briefly, it tells the story of a Peruvian bureaucrat
in his fifties, Dr. Plácido Huamán, who takes advantage of being
sent to a conference in Geneva in order to realize his lifelong
ambition of visiting Paris. Newly arrived in the city, he meets
Solange, who unites the advantages of being young, blond, artistic, and, of course, French. He invites her to dinner, becomes
involved in an amorous adventure that he sees as "a bath of
youthfulness" (1983, 305), and finally falls prey to her cohorts,
a group of ersatz artists, who in their repeatedly frustrated efforts
to steal his money are finally driven to murder him.

The con artists' representation of the Bohemian life is elabo-
rate and easily read; the narrator's representation of Huamán's
experience is abbreviated, hermetic. It is not even clear whether
he is quite ignorant of the band's last ploy or if he in some way
anticipates, even embraces, his approaching end.[2] In the following pages, I shall argue that the ambiguity offers Ribeyro a way
to deal with the utopian projection that underlies this story. Central to *La juventud* is the contrast between the materialistic ethos
that the con game communicates and the intuitions of spiritual
fulfillment, conveyed through Huamán's notion of *la vie de Bohème* and through the series of mysterious images (Notre Dame,
the parks) associated with the idealized vision of earlier societies. Ribeyro fuses a romantic form—the quest—with elements

of parody so that the novella admits affirmative and skeptical readings.

The drama performed by the band of thieves gives Ribeyro an opportunity to ridicule the image of Paris that had long been endemic to Latin American writing.[3] For him, as for Cortázar and Goytisolo, that vision is as much a commodity as the goods sold at the Galeries Lafayette.[4] It is also an almost inescapable part of the experience of tourism in a highly developed area, where, as Dean McCannell argues, the authentic "appears as an infinite regression of stage sets" (1976, 105).[5] The theme of imitation (both as copy and as fake) is insistent in the novella: before she determines to save his money, Solange takes her escort to an expensive restaurant that "meticulously imitated a diner for taxi-drivers" (276) and to the Galeries Lafayette, "an air-conditioned version of an oriental market" (280), where "false geishas" turn out to be "disguised Vietnamese women" (281). None too discriminating a consumer, Huamán is thrilled by both the department store and the restaurant, although he does stop short of purchasing Paradis's execrable tourist scenes and the pornographic works of Jimmi, who claims he caters to the South American taste. It is appropriate that Solange should work as a window dresser, and it is consonant with the reified version of Bohemia they produce that these false artists but perfectly genuine businesspeople should extol "the poetry of poverty" (285) and inveigh against "that materialistic age when, alas, there was no room for real creation" (276).

The group's appropriation of an older code that they then redirect to their own ends is emblematized in the assumption of the name of their leader: Petrus Borel. The original Borel (1809–1859) was known for his outspoken Republicanism and for creating a literature of cruelty that was intended to outrage the bourgeois sensibility. Too, as leader of the *Jeunes France*, he gave what has been described as one of the most notorious parties of the age (Starkie 1954, 91). The fictional Borel's get-together is only a pale imitation—quite literally, since it is not a real party but a spectacle designed to deceive the Peruvian. Politically disengaged, this latter-day Borel realizes the violence that the original espoused only in writing.

In *La juventud* Ribeyro treats *la vie de bohème* as, quite literally, a fraud. Yet, ironically, it is only when he has become involved in the false representation of the city that Huamán feels he has discovered the "real" Paris. That is, the thieves' representation accords with expectations he formed as an adolescent, expectations modeled by his consumption of a certain kind of literature. When Solange conducts him to the tiny studio in the Latin Quarter where he is to enjoy his Parisian idyll, he recognizes the scene:

> as soon as he entered the door he smelled the air of Bohemia that he had dreamed about so often as a young man. This was the typical Parisian garret where someone has a passionate love affair, writes a masterpiece or dies desolate and abandoned. . . .
> "Now, this is Paris," the doctor said. (279)

On his second night in the city, left on his own until the next day by Solange, he tries first to read a pornographic book that he has bought on the quais and then to evoke the nude sculptures he has seen at the Louvre. Finally he falls asleep thinking "that neither art nor literature could take the place of life, that no matter how fleeting and ephemeral she was, a living woman was worth more than all the beautiful statues on earth" (280). Given that Huamán tends to view art as an erotic stimulus, it is perhaps fitting that, when he feels he is living most intensely in the company of Solange, the sensation is effected through the little band's artfully prepared drama. The Left Bank milieu and, at first anyway, the wild party chez Petrus Borel help confirm Huamán's impression that he is finally enjoying the free and easy life of Bohemia as he has imagined it.

The presence of Solange validates his idyll. She is the grisette who will guide him through the labyrinth of the city as Alice did for Gómez Carrillo, who wrote in Treinta años de mi vida that he had initially been so disenchanted with Paris that he preferred to remain in his room reading about the city in the pages of Murger. But Alice (whom he met, incidentally, in the Galeries Lafayette—another eye-opener) soon introduced him to the secret life of the city. In Criollos en París Edwards Bello's Pedro discovers that losing the street-wise Lisette is tantamount to losing Paris. Horacio Oliveira makes the same discovery when La Maga, who has many of the qualities of the grisette-guide, disappears. Possession of the woman, then, implies possession of the city. Like these other grisettes, Solange first offers to act as guide so that Huamán will see "what is really worthwhile" (277), and she soon after takes him to bed with her. The last gesture rounds off "the adventure that he inscribed now, very definitely, in the golden pages of his life" (275). It is hardly casual that when he contemplates the experience Huamán falls back on an image involving literature.

Nor is it casual that in referring to his encounter with Solange he chooses the word "adventure"—simultaneously a brief sexual liaison, a hazardous undertaking, and a type of fiction. The debased version of *la vie de bohème* furnishes *La juventud* with its most obvious literary target. But the story is also informed by another literary predecessor, perhaps inevitable in a narration involving travel: the quest-romance.[6] It is this genre that provides the novella's structure and complicates its meaning. For in spite of the unpromising nature of the hero and his circumstances (which amount to an adventure in the vulgar sense of the word), it is not clear to what extent Ribeyro's appropriation of the quest form is parodic and, therefore, related to the theme of deception,[7] and to what extent it is romantic, suggesting a very different reading, or readings, of the novella.

The heroic quest turns on a series of conventional plot elements: the mysterious call; the hero's solitary journey through a distant and hostile landscape that may be deceptively enticing; the series of tests he must undergo; the encounter, often erotic, with a beautiful woman who may help or hinder him; the search for something—he often does not know exactly what—that will confer meaning on his existence or, in some versions, allow him to enjoy a prolonged youth.

In *La juventud*, the brief references to Huamán's life in Peru present it as a kind of spiritual and emotional wasteland: his wife is "short and skinny" (282); his job involves "obscure, technical work" (282); he is worn out by "years of routine, of impotence, of sumptuous and useless dreams" (283). Finally, the long-awaited call sounds for him: "at last a conference was set up, and there was no way to avoid sending him" (282). Here the strange and dangerous realm is associated in a general way with Paris, which lies "on the other shore"[8] of the Atlantic, but more specifically with the Left Bank—haven of the young—and, later, with the clearing in the forest at Fontainebleau. Barely arrived

in the city, Huamán discovers "the audacity that comes with being in a foreign city, where a person is foreign even to himself"
(276); that is, he has crossed a psychological as well as physical
frontier. (Frye emphasizes the "break in consciousness" or the
alienation from self as a constituent element of romance, 1976,
102.)[9] It is this newfound audacity that prompts him to invite
Solange first for a drink and then for dinner and finally to accept
her offer of a garret apartment, to which he responds: "I don't
want to miss an opportunity. Accepted" (279). When she offers
herself sexually, he accedes "with the eagerness of someone who
finally, even though it is a long time coming, gets his recom-
pense" (283).

The title of the novella, like the river it refers to, unites con-
cepts of time and space. Solange gives a straightforward explanation that "the young, really, are on the other bank" ("la juventud,
realmente, está en la otra ribera," 281). That is, the Parisian
young people gravitate toward the Latin Quarter. This explanation is paralleled by Huamán's earlier comment, "At my age
[fifty], youth is truly on the other bank" ("A esa edad, verdadera-
mente, la juventud está en la otra ribera," 276). His comment
is a spatial expression of a temporal concept, reiterated in the
connection between his youthful reading (time) about Paris
(place).[10] In both cases, the river represents the division between
opposed zones of experience: Right Bank/Left Bank, middle age/
youth. More can be adduced: America/Europe, the known/the
unknown, and, consequently, the safe/the dangerous, everyday
life ("twenty years of routine")/Life ("This is the life," 298), and,
ultimately, life/death.[11]

The tests to which Huamán is subjected involve the gang's
repeated attempts to fleece him. The simulated orgy at Petrus
Borel's represents the most concerted effort to deprive him, without actually resorting to violence, of his funds, and it is also the
culmination of the gang's theatrics. With its carefully cultivated
air of decadence and eroticism, the party assumes an almost
ritualistic character that is hardly essential to the representation
of Bohemia. The guests include a woman called the Medusa,
who dances like "a frenetic dervish" (295), and a drugged dwarf.
One record is repeated so often that it acquires "an hypnotic,
almost sacred, air" (295). Nadine, the dwarf, dances a striptease.
She is followed by Jimmi, painter of erotic scenes and ex-acrobat,

who also strips in order to perform a sword dance, complete with scimitar. In spite, or perhaps because, of the danger, the doctor feels especially invigorated, apparently taking to heart the carpe diem theme, which is voiced hypocritically by both Borel and the Medusa (292 and 298), whose real concern is feathering their nest. "I feel as though I were twenty years old" (292), he comments, and, a bit later, he exclaims, "This is the life. I've never had so much fun" (298).

The hero's initiation into maturity is a common theme in the quest-romance; the parodic elements inherent in the inverted initiation—from middle age to youth—of a portly bureaucrat need not be stressed. What is interesting in the novella, however, is the large area that the notion of parody fails to encompass. The dense pattern of mysterious images and ambiguous gestures gives the doctor's sad story a resonance it would not otherwise have. I am thinking particularly, but not solely, of the evocation of Notre Dame, which presents Huamán with "an enigma, a lost wisdom" (278), and of the series of scenes involving the royal parks that surround the city, culminating in the eerie clearing in Fontainebleau where the doctor is murdered. The significance of these images remains elusive, but they deflect interest from the parody of Bohemia and compromise the parodic intent of the latter-day quest. Linda Hutcheon insists that parody can both reject and long for an earlier literary tradition (32–33). Here the romantic images are so fragmented and the mood so somber that the parodic never entirely subverts the romantic.

Huamán's burst of youthful ardor takes place against the backdrop of the autumnal city. He is strangely drawn to the changing leaves, gorgeous harbingers of seasonal desolation. At Versailles, after touring the palace "respectfully" but without demonstrating great interest, "speechless, struck with emotion, the doctor contemplated the reddish trees" (286–287). At Borel's party, he goes out on the balcony alone to contemplate "the somber foliage of the woods at Vincennes" (292). Later he walks back toward town along the edge of the woods, "inhaling the breath of the foliage" (301). And when he and Solange drive into the forest of Fontainebleau for their picnic,

> the woods grew denser. The foliage was red, bronze, rigid in the windless afternoon.

"Autumn is terrible!" the doctor exclaimed. "I've never seen trees like this." (304)

Perhaps the trees simply represent a bit of exotica for the traveler from a temperate climate. But his strong reaction suggests that the doctor intuits the connection, which is obvious to the reader, between the autumnal trees with their inevitable associations of old age and death and his own situation in life. He may be struck, as well, by the paradoxical beauty of the dying leaves.

Curiously, Huamán's reaction to his first sight of Notre Dame is very similar to his response to the parks. On seeing the trees at Versailles, "he was struck dumb." Faced with the cathedral,

> the doctor was stunned, speechless, not knowing whether to focus on the roughness of the material or the refinement of the forms. The contrast surprised him, and he felt as though he had come upon an enigma, a lost wisdom. (278)

After his visit with Solange, he returns twice on his own to the cathedral: once to climb the tower in order to get a view of the city and once, after his long night at Petrus Borel's, for a last look at "the stubby towers" (301). The doctor, who is out of condition, climbs the four hundred steps "heroically" (290) in order to view the city; that is, he wants to *see*. The medieval cathedral was intended as a picture of the world, a summation of the whole of Christian knowledge (Mâle 1958, ch. 2; Panofsky 1957, 103). Huamán's fascination with the cathedral is related to this notion, and his search for meaning recalls, not without irony, Victor Hugo's Claude Frollo, who studies the cathedral in an effort to grasp "its mystic meaning, the symbolic language lurking under the sculpture on its front . . . the enigma which Notre Dame eternally offers to the understanding" (Hugo 1965, 160).

The connection suggested between the parks and the cathedral is made explicit in the description of the clearing in the forest, where Huamán meets his end: "In the rocks that bordered the clearing, there were openings that led to smaller clearings, distributed like the flamboyant-style chapels in a gothic church" (304). This ritualistic site, like the cathedral, points to the celebration of beliefs that no longer obtain in a culture and an age devoted to conspicuous consumption. It is a landscape as much psychic as physical:[12]

the doctor felt as though he were penetrating an unreal world. They were in a golden, fragrant, winding tunnel that forked and left them in a straight, red tunnel that in turn forked and put them out in a shady avenue that grew wider and wider, finally opening on an enormous, circular clearing that was surrounded by grey and brownish-grey rocks; beyond them, the forest continued. (304)

The "red tunnel" formed by the autumnal trees brings together the motifs of sex and death. It is an "unreal world," the world of the dream—when Paradis appears the doctor comments "I must be dreaming" (307)—and of the unconscious that is characteristic of the romance. This association between the wilderness and the unconscious is traditional, as, too, is the image of the temptress who inhabits the woods and lures the unwary man to his perdition.[13] Appropriately, Huamán reaches the forest at the end of a progression that leads from the orderly park at Versailles through the woods at Vincennes and that corresponds to the crooks' increasingly desperate attempts to get their hands on his dollars and his own increasing sense of pleasure.

When he accepts Solange's last invitation, he is quite aware of her role in the conspiracy and has, in fact, even suggested that she would do well to leave town. There is, then, a strong possibility that he goes on the picnic knowing that something untoward may befall him. In a letter to Wolfgang Luchting, Ribeyro comments that

> What I liked about this story was the way a casual meeting can decide your destiny, the way you are sometimes caught by chance in a mechanism that leads to your own death. (my translation, quoted in Luchting 1983, 149)

The loss of freedom of action, the sense of being spellbound, is a motif related to the romantic hero's experience of the demonic world.[14] But there is also a degree of willfulness on Huamán's part. In the same letter, Ribeyro draws attention to "the theme of the 'fatal choice' [which appears] in filigree. The doctor was aware of something, but he decides to go ahead with it" (149). An important part of the "mechanism" that imprisons Huamán, then, is his own determination to see the adventure through.

No matter what the doctor intuits about his fate, he is clearly convinced that he has miraculously recuperated his youth: "For me, this has been, more than anything else, a bath of youth-fulness. I told you once that for me youth was on the other bank of the river. This time I've reached that bank" (305). After finish-ing off the bread and wine, he eats an apple and then falls on Solange, "voraciously, roughly" (306). The images of the apple, the erotic encounter, the forest setting, the circular clearing: all suggest the recovery of the lost center, the paradisiacal state of wholeness.

It is, of course, brief. Huamán's eagerness to "consume" So-lange—she is "edible" (275) and "tasty" (277), and he throws himself on her "voraciously" (306)—indicate that he intuits as much. Woman and apple are both forbidden fruit; they bring fulfillment and knowledge, but also the expulsion from paradise and death. Huamán glimpses nightingales and larks just as he dies. The return to the womb, implied in the expression "a bath of youthfulness" and the shape of the clearing, leads, inevitably, to annihilation. In the mythical quest, once his adventure has ended, the transformed hero returns home bearing a boon that will restore mankind (Campbell 1949, 246). There is no such return here. Huamán's epiphany is purely individual. The com-munity of endeavor involved in the construction of Notre Dame, the harmonious relation between man and nature suggested in the parks, and the belief in a transcendent reality expressed in both the cathedral and the clearing belong to an idealized view of a different age.

Various indicators point to this nostalgia for a golden age. The name Paradis needs no comment—he pulls the trigger—but other names are important as well.[15] The doctor's immediately calls to mind the frustrated utopian Huamán Poma de Ayala, who described the by then dismantled Incan Empire as an ideal state. That Plácido Huamán should transfer the ideal to nineteenth-century Paris reveals a subtler and, in some ways, more destructive phase of colonialism.

The original Petrus Borel railed constantly against the vulgar-ity and materialism of Bohemian Paris—an obvious irony here—and finally migrated to the newly conquered Algeria, where he took on a job as colonial supervisor and built himself a gothic folly named Castel de la Haulte Pensée. The pseudo-Borel is an Arab, come to prey on the metropolis (much as Garro's Mexicans do in *Reencuentro de personajes*). This repetition, incidentally, is part of the air of magic that characterizes romance, and it is worth noting that the French Solange appears to be more victim than instigator—there is even a suggestion that, like a spellbound princess, she looks to Huamán for release (302). The Arab Borel appropriates the mythos of Bohemian Paris, but he puts it to the service of an ethos embodied in the Galeries Lafayette, that "palace of consumption" (281).

The opposition between the romantic view that attempts to discern the outlines of the sacred behind the appurtenances of everyday life—seeing—and the commercial that privileges not exactly the appurtenances but the price they will fetch and the value they will confer—being seen—is conveyed through a series of contrasting images. The windows of the tower of Notre Dame, along with the many other references to windows throughout the novella—of the attic apartment (referred to repeatedly), of the bar (curtained) where Huamán meets Paradis and Jimmi and behind which they first plan to fleece him, of Versailles, of Borel's apartment, of the wretched suburbs Solange drives through on the way to Fontainebleau, of the car with Borel inside—all hint at the importance of perception. These windows are opposed to shopwindows, which also figure large in the story. The shopwindows Solange arranges; the café where she and Huamán first meet that is like a shopwindow (275); the show windows at the Galeries Lafayette and in the antique shop where Solange admires the impossibly expensive desk, a kind of icon of consumerism (as well as a vestige of the ancien régime); the garret window that reflects Solange posing in her new coat like a mannequin—all of them present a carefully calculated vision of life intended to take in potential customers. The café is a place where Solange can shop for prospective targets, but also where tourists, like the doctor, can shop for local women.

Perhaps the neatest conjunction of the romantic and the modern occurs in the last scene, with the intrusion of the newspaper in the mysterious clearing. The paper that serves as tablecloth for the picnic and that Solange stares at persistently during lunch and the paper Borel reads while he waits in the car imply that the rhythm of life in the outside world goes on unchanged even though Huamán has reached a still point. This rhythm depends on the succession of events and not on the change in seasons that marks bucolic time. A phenomenon that sprang out of the Bohemian period, the newspaper caters to a taste for the individual and the temporary rather than the universal and the permanent. Even the layout of the newspaper conspires to the same end. The columns are juxtaposed with no attempt to relate the news covered, conveying a vision that Marshall McLuhan calls "front page cubism" (1967, 3); whereas the clearing appeals to a need for what is eternal, harmonious and complete. The clearing and the cathedral—that "book of stone" (Hugo 1965, 175), with its message of faith—will be superseded by the printing press, as Hugo points out in *Notre Dame de Paris* (1965, 173–188), itself a product of the early years of the newspaper. The doctor will finally be reduced to a column or half-column in the papers back home, and the newspapers Solange and Borel are reading will probably be used to feed the flames that destroy his corpse. The man whose literary expectations led him astray will be consumed in and by print.

The antithetical notions of comsumption and of perception meet in Huamán, who is bemused by an intuition of some other meaning in the itinerary of his little adventure but also intent on consuming Solange and with her the experience she represents. Whether for him that experience involves only the Parisian affair that he expects to inscribe in "the golden pages of his life" (275)—part of a *collection* of vital experiences that would assume the "congealed state" of the commodity (Debord 1977, 35)—or whether it entails some realization of his fate is never quite clear.

Ribeyro once remarked in an interview that

> with a little patience, more could be found in my work than has been found so far. What? Of course, I'm not going to say. I'll act like that character in Henry James's "The Figure in the Carpet," the one who tortures a critic all his life, inviting him to discover "the figure in the carpet" in his work, only to leave him at the end wondering if there really had been a figure. (1977, 59)

In *La juventud*, the laconic narration and the stubborn ambiguity allow Ribeyro simultaneously to indulge in and deny the romantic view. By fusing an archaizing form (the quest-romance) with elements of parody and a strong undercurrent of irony, Ribeyro conveys both longing and skepticism, the nostalgia for transcendent meaning and the suspicion that in the contemporary world meaning is only contingent. The tendency to believe that the "old values" once conferred meaning is probably delusory and perhaps even dangerous, but the conviction that meaning *should* exist is inescapable. There is a sense that the story is gathering itself for a revelation that the reader, at least, never experiences and yet continues to search for, even demand, and that the author has taken pains to elide.

4
At Home Abroad, Abroad at Home: *El recurso del método*

In THE OPENING SCENE OF ALEJO CARPENTIER'S *EL RECURSO DEL MÉTODO* (*Reasons of State*),[1] the Prime Minister awakens in his Paris home and, like the young protagonist in *A la Recherche du temps perdu*, recalls the beds in which he has awakened in the past— the child's experience here is transformed into an inventory of the rooms in the dictator's favorite brothel. On arising, he surveys his collection of paintings and sculpture. And then, a few pages later, he engages in a lengthy discussion of French writers and composers (including Proust's Vinteuil) with the Illustrious Academic, who has dropped by in hopes that he can flog the manuscripts of two plays—one a drama of conscience,[2] the other an historical drama. He ends the visit by reciting a stanza from Hugo's "A l'Arc de Triomphe."

Insistent throughout this novel, the copious allusions to literature, the use of ekphrases, the incorporation of extraneous texts and of characters from other works: all appear to serve a mimetic function, conveying the atmosphere of Belle Epoque Paris and delineating the character of the Head of State, but they are finally subversive, drawing our attention away from what is represented to how it is represented. Here the use of period detail, one of the most common strategies for creating a sense of the past, is so excessive that it verges on the parodic. In passages like this one, the disproportionate attention paid to the absurd detail sends up any notion of a history of everyday life:

> The monks in all the German hygroscopes had their hoods permanently thrown back on their necks; the peasant with the umbrella of Swiss hygroscopes remained hidden in his rustic alpine chalet,

while that personification of fine weather, the girl with a red apron, was out all the time. (1976, 96; 107)[3]

The novel is profuse in detail. It proceeds by a strategy of repetition, holding the mirror not to nature but to itself and to other texts. It is informed by this tension between the desire for presence—the need to recapture time and place—and the consciousness of absence that leads to both the piling on of detail in an *horror vacui* and the temptation to point defiantly at the process of creation.[4]

El recurso is in continuous oscillation between these two impulses, so that the same gesture that lays bare the artifice becomes part of its density—and vice versa. Unstable, too, is the locus of value, which fluctuates between France and America, following the mental as well as physical discursions of the peripatetic dictator. The two movements are connected. The dictator is a performer, a source of authority that has no ground; the narration is a performance that may reflect nothing but itself. The subject of this chapter will be the alternation between the kind of representation that attempts to elide the process of mediation and the kind that plays up that process. The chapter is also concerned with the dispersal of meaning, which suggests that there is, ultimately, no authoritative source of truth. Such a tendency is disturbing in a novel purporting to communicate a moment typical of early twentieth-century Latin American history that is part of a greater historical process—world revolution, presumably real. I shall take up this point toward the end of these pages.

Carpentier has written that in the great European cities, "the backdrops are packaged . . . their style is fixed forever" (my translation, 1964, 16–17). He exploits this potentially stultifying notion in *El recurso* to evoke the period and suggest the dreams of his *rastaquouère* head of a state, and also to adumbrate the relationship between art and history. His vision of Paris unfolds under the sign of stasis. For the dictator, blissfully unaware that the Great War will put an end to the Belle Epoque, the city is an unchanging utopia where he can cultivate the good life after the bounce and scramble of his journey up the social ladder. His mansion on the Rue du Tilsitt is both an extension of his ideal self and a reduction of his idealized view of Paris. It mediates between the parvenu Prime Minister and the city, serving to naturalize his appearance in a social circle valued precisely for its reputation of being impenetrable and unchangeable.[5]

Much of the imagery in the opening pages of the novel suggests that here the dictator has found his true center: he arises in the morning and advances "towards the light" (10; 11), opening the curtain to gaze out on the Arc de Triomphe, with its sense of promise. He is the center of attention of a series of efficient attendants and is encircled, quite literally, by his collection of art. His personal progress from the swamps of Surgidero de la Verónica to the great boulevards where he feels he has finally achieved the goal of becoming—this is the way he puts it—a person (303; 334) is paralleled by the view of history embodied in this collection. With the exceptions of the Elstir (to be discussed later) and the view of Nueva Córdoba,[6] the artworks convey an exalted conception of history, leading from Gérôme's gladiators through Jean-Paul Laurens's crusaders to Rude's Marseillaise (clearly visible from the window and included as the last item in the inventory), and an idealized sense of the present time and place: early twentieth-century Paris, culmination of centuries of progress.[7]

The collection provides an index to mainstream French taste in the prewar period; academic paintings like these were prized for what was considered to be their faithful representation of the subject. Raymond Rudorff comments that "it was believed that there was only one way to paint a picture" (1972, 97–98). The inference is that there was also only one way to view reality. This popular form of Cartesianism that suggests that reality is both readily apprehensible to and shared by right-thinking individuals is contravened throughout the novel, where different realities are juxtaposed and all prove to be equally elusive. What seems obvious on one side of the Atlantic may not be self-evident on the other. According to Rudorff, the kind of art represented in the dictator's collection was an art designed to "instruct, adorn, edify and exalt," but not to question, and certainly not to disturb (97). It remained curiously unaware of the profound changes that were being forged in Western art right underneath its nose:

Most of the critics, the public and buyers generally agreed that French art had reached an ideal state and was destined to continue as before, with each new generation of artists faithfully adhering to established styles and standards. (98)

Among the affluent living in Paris at the time, the consensus seems to have been that contemporary life, like contemporary art, had reached a state of perfection that it was hoped might be prolonged indefinitely by repetition.

The notion of an ideal stasis, embodied in the mansion with its comforting daily rituals and its carefully cultivated atmosphere of continuity and distinction, is parodied in the dictator's second Parisian home: the brothel run by Madame Yvonne. Duplicated, the mansion no longer functions as the center of value. The ostentatious theatricality that is the brothel's hallmark exposes the self-consciousness with which the scene on the Rue du Tilsitt is staged. There is more: Madame Yvonne, animating spirit of the brothel, is a figure suspiciously like the dictator. A self-made woman who hovers on the edge of gentility, she manipulates an exquisite sense of decorum and a French "which passed from Port Royal to the argot of Bruant, according to circumstances and the condition of the client—much like my French which was part Montesquieu, part *Nini-peau-de-chien*," her customer muses (12–13; 14).

As though to remind us of the brothel's parodic function—duplication with an ironic difference—there is in it a "Palace of Mirrors." There, we are told in a baroque simile, the dictator has seen himself in every physical position so often that those images are impressed on his memory, "just as an album of family photographs catalogues the gestures, attitudes and clothes of the best days of one's life" (12; 14). Temporal movement is fixed in the image, and the love of family is mirrored in a different kind of transaction.

In the brothel, time seems to stand still. A prostitute dressed as a bride "was deflowered four or five times a night" (12; 13). One of the rooms is a copy of a berth on the sleeping car of a train, its run "eternally at a standstill" (11; 13). Another is a replica of a stateroom on the *Titanic*, hovering on the edge of a disaster always imminent yet never realized except in *la petite mort* that is effectively the journey's end. Enshrined in yet another room is the specially designed armchair to which Edward VII accommodated his erotic exertions—a paradox of sedentary activity. In the carefully preserved armchair, the train and *Titanic* rooms, the ever-virgin prostitute, and the metaphorical photo album, the flow of history is arrested, as it is on the printed page and in the Prime Minister's collection of paintings, where succession is laid out in a physical space that admits repeated readings or viewings. The parodic exaggeration of Madame Yvonne's efforts to defy the passage of time reminds us that, viewed as real life, theirs is a precarious utopia. It is only through art that an immutable present can be achieved. But this is the present tense of the imagination, not of the world.

A kind of perpetuity has been achieved, of course, by the Prime Minister's most outrageous double: the globe-trotting mummy, whose transatlantic misadventures recall Evita's. The mummy is part of the pattern of images that opposes the clean, well-lighted house on the rue du Tilsitt, a projection of the Prime Minister's ideal self, to the dark cave, most basic of refuges, which is both womb and tomb: origin and end. The mummy has a definite commodity value, but the fascination it exercises over the Prime Minister has little to do with cultural prestige. Its enigmatic presence enfolds both the dark past of America and the dark future—deposition and death—that awaits his interlocutor. The identification between the mummified cacique and the dictator is established in parallel scenes: one in which the Head of State poses for his tailor, noting, "I turn around, like a mannequin, stopping at angles where my figure appears in a favorable light" (14; 16),[8] and another in which the mummy is posed for photographs—"There it was photographed from every angle" (93; 104). Virtually the last comment the dictator ever makes is addressed to the figure, now encased in glass in the Trocadero: "Don't complain, you bastard, I took you out of your mud and turned you into a person" (303; 334).

Becoming a person, according to the standard set by Paris, has been the goal of the Prime Minister's life. But in the end, effectively confined to the dark upper reaches of his mansion while Ofelia reigns in the reception rooms, the Ex, as he calls himself after being deposed, is as out of place in the city of his dreams as the mummy in the Trocadero. Both are reduced to curiosities. The house that once mediated between him and Paris is now closed in upon itself; like the cave, the attic has no view. As he approaches death, the Ex regresses toward childhood, and here, too, he is preceded by the mummy, perenially curled in a fetal position. His effort to confound both time and space through a culinary return to a lost America—the dainty madeleine transmogrified into gargantuan feasts involving tamales, *chicharrones*, and great quantities of *caña*—is delusory. Only in Père Lachaise is the utopian ideal of the perfect present realized. Emblematically, the Ex—now doubly Ex—is interred between the tombs of Baudelaire and General Aupic and the tomb of Porfirio Díaz; that is, somewhere between the pen and the sword, between poetry and history—in other words, in the never-never land of fiction.

The vision of a lost America superimposed on Paris is not just a product of the dictator's dotage. Consistently in this novel, Carpentier represents Paris in relation to America. On the first page, for example, just as one series of images suggests that the dictator has found his center, another hints at something quite different. We are told that he awakes in his hammock "with the feeling of being *there*." He imagines Elmira sleeping "in the darkness of the other hemisphere." He looks out on a view where, "instead of a volcano—the snow-covered, majestic, remote, ancient Home of the Gods"—he spots the house belonging to Porfirio Díaz's minister of finance, Yves Limantour, with whom he discusses "our problems." He accepts coffee brought in on a tray made of "thick, beautiful silver from my mines," coffee that is "Bien fort comme il l'aime. A la façon de lá-bas" (9–10; 11). It is not simply a question of economic dependence. It is that, like the conquistadores, who could apprehend the New World only in terms of Europe, the Prime Minister's appreciation of *his* New World depends on a constant awareness of the other side for meaning. It is tempting to see this tendency as a commentary on representation in which presence must be defined by absence and the familiar provides the only entry point for the unfamiliar.[9]

Of course, back home, the Prime Minister measures the capital by a European standard, exulting in its pell-mell dash to catch up with the architecture and high life of Paris at the same time that he laments the loss of familiar views. These shifts in the locus of value depend on a series of antinomies that suggest the distinction between civilization and barbarism, only to complicate the terms until the neat divider no longer serves. A case in point is the relationship between the Arc de Triomphe and the tutelary volcano. As it is set up on the first page of the novel, the relationship opposes nature to artifice and an ancient pagan cult to one of the crowning monuments of the Capital of Reason. But the slumbering volcano also represents the outrage of an oppressed people. The arch, intended to commemorate the French Republic's revolutionary wars, has come to stand for a sense of patriotism of marked rightest tendencies that is not notably rational, the kind espoused by the Illustrious Academic.[10] Rude's Marseillaise, the bas-relief that adorns one of the sides, represents the Republic going into war to defend its freedom, but it reminds the Prime Minister of the caudillos, motivated by greed and the desire for power. Hugo's "A l'Arc de Triomphe," a stanza of which the Prime Minister recites for the Illustrious Academic, suggests the same sort of smug and overblown patriotism. But there is more: in the same poem (stanzas the leader does not recite), Hugo refers to the monuments of unjust nations—so unlike those of France, he points out—whose foundations conceal a tyrant's crimes. The poet predicts that these bloodstained monuments will not withstand the passage of time because a just god will command nature to take them over again (1855, 2:215).[11] Years later in the homeland, economic shortages and political unrest bring about the partial collapse of the city, presumably including the dictator's chief monuments—the Capitol and the Model Prison, which contains corpses of suspected enemies encased in the poured concrete foundation.

The Arc also reflects the dictator's personal relationship with Paris. Monumental embodiment of the ambitions of a more illustrious outsider—the Corsican, Napoleon—it serves him as a fixed point of reference. When he is immersed in furious modernization back at home, he evokes its image as a comforting reminder that Paris will always be Paris. However, when the Prime Minister's Parisian acquaintances begin to snub him, he longs to see the German army marching victorious through its gates, and in his perception the erstwhile solid structure grows or shrinks according to the news from the front. Much later, the Arc serves the Mayorala as a landmark for her own itinerary of Paris. Blissfully unaware of its historic significance, she sails through it every day on her way to the Madeleine (a little joke here), where she buys the cane syrup indispensable to their nostalgic feasts. In this roundabout way, the Arc finally marks both the defeat of the Prime Minister's dream of conquering "le tout Paris" and his emotional regression to things American. In a parallel image, his defeat has been foreshadowed by the volcano, which, lost in the welter of modernization,

> was less a volcano—less even the abode of the Ancient Gods—when on misty mornings its majestic presence seemed to insinuate itself, with the modesty of a humiliated king, a monarch without a court, above the dense clouds of smoke sent up by four tall chimneys from the recently inaugurated Central Electricity Company. (135–36; 151–52).

Carpentier uses the volcano and the arch, then, to explore clichés of national identity that turn out to be misleading. He reproduces other national clichés throughout the text, without necessarily questioning them. Often they form part of hilarious vignettes. The description of the German crews that are interned when their ships are captured, for example, is a catalog of received ideas:

> [some of them built] pretty chalets in the Rhenish style, while others planted gladioli and rolled the ground to make tennis-courts. Three weeks later the farm had became a model estate. There was a library, with the poems of Heinrich Heine and even of the socialist Dehmel. Of course it lacked women, but many of them had no need of them, being homosexual on the whole. . . . And as they were very musical, they made an orchestra from the instruments they had brought on board ship, and began to play the lesser works of Haydn, Mendelssohn and Raff, his *Cavatina* in particular. (146; 163)

When these cultural caricatures are rendered from the Prime Minister's or the Illustrious Academic's viewpoint, a mimetic function can be adduced: they convey the characters' prejudices. But this is only sometimes the case. They are often presented from what purports to be an objective point of view. No matter what the narrative position, they *always* call our attention to the act of fabrication.

In the essay cited earlier, Carpentier argues that the challenge confronting American novelists is to inscribe the physiognomy of their cities on world literature (1964, 14). The home scenes in *El recurso* are not situated in Havana or Caracas, but in the unnamed capital of an unnamed country that synthesizes American geography and uses. They provide a schema for the representation of a great number of Latin American cities without actually representing any one city, like the Renaissance pattern books that furnished artists with a general vocabulary of images to be used as a basis for individual representations. By dint of the sort of cultural reductionism that characterizes his national caricatures, Carpentier presents an America viewed from a perspective that fails to differentiate between disparate geographical areas and cultural and linguistic spheres. It is presented from a European perspective, like Conrad's Costagüana and Valle Inclán's Zamalpoa. Quintessentially American, Carpentier's country is also the kind of wonderland that exists only on the page. His insistence on the theatrical, which is especially marked in his description of the capital, is of course related to the wartime economic boom that works dramatic changes in the cityscape almost overnight—that is, it functions as mimesis. But it may also be a tongue-in-cheek reminder that "the Opera-City, the Capital of Fiction" (176; 195) is exactly that.

In this dialectic of representation that playfully counters mimesis with poesis, *El recurso* contests the Cartesian view that the proper use of language corresponds precisely to a universal rational method, which in turn adequately represents the underlying order of nature. Such a view insists that meaning is fixed and language is both transparent and stable; that is, it denies the play of ambiguity and the eccentric. Timothy J. Reiss argues that this attitude, which became widespread by the 1740s, is the result of a fundamentally political activity directed to the stabilizing of civil society:

> The tetrad of Bacon, Galileo, Hobbes, and Descartes . . . saw method, language, natural philosophy, and political order as forming a single network. The new concept of poetical representation becomes the focal point organizing this network of relations. (1982, 224)

Accordingly, the king is viewed as both "the principal poet of his country and the unique sovereign. He brings political and linguistic stability" (229). The parodic inversion of Descartes's thinking signaled in the title of *El recurso* involves not only the ironic application of Cartesian principles to the least Cartesian of worlds and the least Cartesian of leaders while revealing the inherent dangerousness of Descartes's *morale provisoire*.[12] It also embraces Descartes's notions about language and representation. As his country's chief orator, if not poet, the dictator (i.e., one who dictates—an idea also explored throughout Roa Bastos's *Yo el Supremo*) certainly has a gift for the gab. But his taste in rhetoric tends toward the baroque; it is richly embroidered with

> "swords of Damocles", "crossing the Rubicon", trumpets of Jericho, Cyranos, Tartarins and Clavileños, all mixed up together with lofty palm-trees, solitary condors and white pelicans. (43; 47–48)

Fond of quotation, the Head of State lards his speech with literary allusions and is not above lifting material when it suits him, as he does for the inauguration of the new capitol, borrowing in that instance from Renan. In this parody of his own writing, Carpentier provides the dictator with a style that points not toward an underlying order clear to anyone possessed of common sense, such as Descartes prescribed, but to the language itself or to other texts. His speech, then, does not remit the listener (or reader) to a universal system of referents, but rather it allows for the play of meaning. It accords well with the tropical taste of his countrymen and denies the efficacy of a universal grammar. It de-centers the Cartesian universe while it affirms the difference—linguistic and cultural—of the periphery.

This use of language opens up a multivalent discourse, asserting the value of disparate voices, but it also is subject to abuse. Taking advantage of the divorce between signifier and signified, the dictator manipulates language for his own ends. He meets every crisis with a flood of decrees and pronouncements, until, at one point, words fail him, their divorce from the current situation made too blatant even for him:

> ... nothing about *Liberty*—with the jails full of political prisoners. ... Nothing about *Virtues*—when he was known to be the owner of the richest businesses in the country. No *Legitimate Rights*—since he ignored them whenever they conflicted with his own personal jurisprudence. His vocabulary was decidedly narrowing. (111; 123)

Hardly prone to soul-searching, he deals with the situation simply by finding a new set of words, the "Holy Crusade of Latinity" (114; 126), which have the great virtue of signifying nothing. González Echevarría argues that the Head of State's official pronouncements are "a parody of political rhetoric in which speech is the product of a muddled mind" (1985, 73). However, the novel makes it clear that the dictator uses language quite consciously to achieve his own ends. To wit:

> he knew that such an artificial language had created a style which was part of his image, and that the use of words, adjectives and unusual epithets seldom understood by his hearers, far from being prejudicial, flattered some atavistic taste of theirs for what was precious and flowery. (44; 48)

González Echevarría points out that Carpentier "demystifies the notion of authority by identifying himself with the dictator" since "one cannot but see in the music-loving, erudite First Magistrate, who divides his life between Latin America and Paris, a parody of Carpentier himself" (73). However, he does not make the connection between their rhetorical styles. Yet, both employ a polyphonic discourse in which immediacy gives way to allusion, and meaning becomes meanings that are sometimes incompatible. What suits the dictator's ends—confounding his adversaries, impressing his friends—is sometimes less apt for the novelist, who does not always manage to synthesize the contradictory impulses that inform his narrative.

Carpentier writes against a background of literature. In the essay cited earlier, he notes, tellingly,

> it is hard to bring something out about a place that has not already been written about in books and in letters, that has not been equipped with a catalog of the emotions, connections and expressions of admiration it provokes. (my translation, 1964, 18)

The brillant descriptions of the rapidly modernized capital are inspired not only by his research into American documents of the period and his own experiences. They are also, I suspect, inspired by Baudelaire's evocation in "Le Cygne" of the violent disruptions wrought in mid-nineteenth-century Paris by the de-

molition of the medieval city and the construction of Haussmann's boulevards:

> Yet in my mind I still can see the booths;
> The heaps of brick and rough-hewn capitals;
> The grass; the stones all over-green with moss;
> The débris, and the square-set heaps of tiles. (1958, 78)

Carpentier evokes the site of the new capital during the periods of inactivity brought on by the misappropriation of funds
as "this strange chaotic landscape of marbles, half-finished met-
opes, truncated pillars, blocks of stone between cement and
sand" (154; 159), where a skating rink is opened and various
circus shows are held, including an exhibition of animals, like
the menagerie from which Baudelaire's swan has escaped. Carpentier's tone is amused; Baudelaire's melancholy, almost tragic.
The sense of being in exile even at home is the subject of Baudelaire's poem and is, in part, brought on by the rapid transformations in the urban scene—"Old Paris is no more (a town, alas, /
Changes more quickly than man's heart may change)" (79). This
sense is reflected onto the Prime Minister, who is saddened by
the expansion that he himself has promoted, and who winds up
feeling cut off from the scenes he has loved:

> As he watched the metropolis grow and grow, the Head of State
> was sometimes worried by the changes in the view from the Palace
> windows. He was himself involved in a real-estate business . . .
> whose buildings were destroying the panorama for so long part of
> his life, so that when his attention was suddenly drawn to some
> alteration in it . . . he started as if at some evil omen. . . . (135–36;
> 151)

The presence of another author backstage, so to speak, in this
scene is characteristic of the novel as a whole, which is created
against a scrim of other texts. Few moments are not reminiscent
of something else. Even the scene in the mummy's cave, where
the dictator comes face to face with the prehistoric past, is mediated through literary and operatic allusions. In response to the
storm that tears down their tents, the Head of State quotes from
King Lear, and Doctor Peralta answers with the Puñal del godo.
The cavern where they take shelter reminds the leader of one of

the sets in *Pelléas et Mélisande*, which he has just seen in New York. And it inspires Colonel Hoffmann to attempt an aria from *Siegfried* because it brings to mind the grottoes frequented by Alberich and Mime.

It is true that the bizarre dislocations that mark the trajectory of the imaginary capital are grounded in historical fact: many American cities underwent virtually the same transformations. Angel Rama writes that "any amused reader of *Social*, a magazine that catered to Havana high society from 1918 to 1936, would recognize and relive that time [in the pages of Carpentier's novel]" (my translation, 1976, 43). Urged, probably, by the nostalgic impulse to recapture a past remembered from his youth, as well as by a sense of historical consciousness, Carpentier creates a convincingly real world, only to remind the reader teasingly that what he purveys here is a product of the imagination.

The passages describing the arrival of the opera, the design and construction of the capitol and, especially, the preparations for the dedication of the capitol (conveyed in a scene out of Cecil B. De Mille), which involves painting over the wilted leaves of the newly planted trees: all of these sections focus on the process rather than the product. Not only in the actual opera sets but also in the capitol, the spruced-up palms, and the fanciful mansions of the newly rich, the end result is more theatrical than solid, more illusion (or *allusion*) than concrete construction. The capitol building is a copy of the capitol in Washington, and the other new constructions are

> theatrically got up in Mediaeval, Renaissance or Hollywood-Andalusian colour-schemes, and without the smallest connection with the country's history, or else in large buildings aping the Second Empire style of the Boulevard Haussman. The new Central Post Office had a superb Big Ben. The new head Police Station was a Temple from Luxor in eau-de-nil. The country house of the Chancellor of the Exchequer was a pretty miniature Schönbrunn. The President of the Chamber kept his mistress in a little Abbaye de Cluny, swathed in imported ivy. (175; 195)

This sort of description suggests the cultural and, ultimately, economic insubstantiality of the modernized capital—that is, it is representational. But it also foregrounds the *process* of creating an illusion, whether in masonry or in words.

Overtly fictive is the passage that correlates the plummeting price of sugar with the progress of the opera season, a passage modeled on events that took place in the summer of 1920 during Caruso's stay in Havana. Carpentier writes:

> Our sugar was fetching 23 centavos a pound when Nicoletti-Korman, a magnificent devil, was sending up prayers to the Golden Calf. With the North American anthem in the first act of *Madame Butterfly*, it fell to 17.20. It was quoted at 11.35 during *Thais*. . . . On the disastrous day of *Rigoletto*—and hunchbacks are supposed to bring good luck—it fell to 8.40. The cheating at cards in the fourth act of *Manon* hastened the collapse, which with the catastrophe of *Aida*, left us at 5.22. (185; 205)

What begins here as a witty means of bringing together two disparate phenomena—the opera season and the sugar disaster—ends by suggesting a cause-and-effect relationship between the operatic and the economic tragedies that operates according to the law of sympathetic magic, which, as Borges points out, is characteristic of fiction.[13] The violent yoking together of food, clothing, language, and uses, typical of very different regions, has the same effect, providing a constant reminder to the American, if not the European, reader that the homeland is an imaginary construct.

A more disquieting reminder of that fact is the inclusion in a list detailing the instruments of torture used in local police stations of "corn-cobs—these were for women" (164; 183). The playful allusion to Faulkner's *Sanctuary*, in which the impotent villain rapes the young woman he has abducted with just that object, tends to deflect meaning, pointing not toward a circumstantial reality, but toward another text. The inference, probably unintentional but nonetheless inevitable, is that the dictator's methods are part of the writer's resources, a timeless literary motif.

The protagonist's own reality is put in doubt in the very first chapter of the novel, where we are told that he owns a painting by Elstir, listens to music by Vinteuil, and cultivates the acquaintance of Madame Verdurin. The inclusion of these figures out of *A la recherche du temps perdu* breaks the frame of what purports to be a true history, exposing its basis in literature.[14] The same thing is implied by the Ex's last words, cribbed from Augustus Caesar: "Acta est fabula" (338), "the play is finished." In other words, like the plot that chronicles it, his life has been an illusion, a shadow of other lives.[15] In their conversation, the Student and Julio Antonio Mella echo another version of the line—Joseph de Maistre's:

> How many times, since that horrifying revolution and the fatal wars it provoked, have we had all the reason in the world to say: *Acta est fabula,* and yet the same scene goes on and on! (My translation, *Fleurs* n.d., 9).

Whereas Maistre, from his position on the extreme right, wrote lamenting the excesses of the French Revolution and the Napoleonic Wars, the Student and Mella give the images a very different idealogical application. But perhaps the repetition is as important as the difference:

> "We've just got rid of a dictator," said the Student. "But the struggle goes on, because our enemies are the same as before. The curtain has gone down on the first act, and very long it was. Now we're in the middle of the second, which in spite of new scenery and lighting, is very like the first. . . ."
> "That's a sight we've been seeing repeated for the last hundred years."
> "Until the public gets tired of seeing the same thing." (295–96; 326–327)

Hanging in both the mansion on the Rue du Tilsitt and in the country house at Marbella are seascapes painted by Elstir. Of these seascapes, which he refers to as almost mirages, Proust's narrator writes, "the sea's "reflections had almost more solidity and reality than the floating hulls, vaporised by an effect of the sunlight" (1934, 1:630). Again, the inference is the same: the protagonist, the other characters, the time and place and series of events, all of which seem so full of life, so convincing, are reflections of something else. But that something else regresses into literature, so that the image of an instrument of torture calls to mind not a real instrument but an allusion in another novel to an instrument of torture. And the description of a painting brings to mind not the image of a painting but another description of a painting in another work of literature.

The point here is not that the Prime Minister is "unreal" because he is inauthentic and his life a farce. Instead, issues of this sort are dissolved into the continuum of literature. From the historical and political perspective, the tendency is disturbing. In her dicussion of what she calls historiographic metafiction, Linda Hutcheon writes that the novels in this group do not question the existence of an objective reality, but rather they question our ability to understand it unproblematically (1989, 81–82). They take as explicit theme "the desire for and suspicion of narrative mastery," as, for example, does Yo el Supremo, which is structured around this conflict (64). In El recurso the subject is not under discussion. The novel ostensibly presents a significant period in the development of the Latin American republics, while it covertly undermines the notion that history is a shaping force in the narrative and, by extension, casts doubt on the significance of history in the life of that continent or human life in general. Strictly speaking, El recurso is not a historical novel since it relates events that are typical rather than actual, but it ostensibly effects what Frederic Jameson calls "the concept of history" (1984, 180). Actually, it remits the reader to a realm that lies close to the circular ruins of Borges. Carpentier seems to want things both ways—to represent a significant external reality and to expose that representation as a fiction. Yet this exposure is effected in such a way that it subverts confidence not only in the representation but in the reality itself.

In an emblematic scene near the end of the novel, the deposed dictator, together with Elmira and Mendoza, pauses at Notre Dame de Paris at the same moment that the Student, en route to the First World Congress against Colonial and Imperialist Politics in Brussels, stops there. Their very different reactions to the cathedral suggest the two visions of experience that the novel, as I see it, intends to convey. The Ex uses the cathedral as a point of departure to recount "true stories" (292; 323) straight out of Hugo to the admiring Elmira[16]; the Student focuses instead on the sweeping vertical lines of the structure and the conception of history communicated in the great roseate windows. In other words, the dictator is concerned with the anecdote, the representation, and he makes no distinction between fiction and history. The Student takes the long view and sees the structure that supports the decoration, the vision of life that gave birth to the cathedral. He relates that vision to his own (Marxist) view of history as leading, ultimately if not easily, toward a terrestrial paradise.

This episode suggests that Carpentier, like Proust, conceived of his novel as a cathedral.[17] The plot centers on the Prime Minister (tragedy reduced to the level of farce), analogous to the grotesque figures carved on the tympanun and the lintels. The plot involves the Student and the evolution of political consciousness among the people (comic), representative of the structure of the cathedral itself.[18] Such a reading of the novel would align it with what Jameson describes as the "national allegory":

> Third-world texts, even those which are seemingly private and invested with a properly libidinal dynamic—necessarily project a political dimension in the form of the national allegory: *the story of the private individual destiny is always an allegory of the embattled situation of the public third-world culture and society.* (1986, 69)

In theory, Carpentier's novel works well within this schema; the use of titles instead of names for the most important characters directs the reader's attention to the novel's allegorical dimension.[19] In fact, the passages invoking the Student are programmatic and thin, while the novel's real interest is concentrated on the play of "true stories" that surround the figure of the dictator and that, as I have suggested, tend to deny the possibility of history. Opposed to Notre Dame is the house of another dame: Madame Yvonne's brothel, that favorite hangout of the Head of State. It is from this vantage point that Carpentier—who was a man of about the Prime Minister's age when the novel was written, and like him, a *rastaquouère* and a dictator wielding an authority based on the power of the word—gives the reader a knowing wink. With its hall of mirrors, with its reduction of time to space and history to repetition, this edifice is a far better emblem than the cathedral of *El recurso del método*.

5

La Chambre voisine: Latin America and Paris in *Una familia lejana*

Europe is literally the creation of the Third World.
—Frantz Fanon (1968, 102)

OF THESE SPANISH AMERICAN NOVELS THAT TAKE PLACE IN PARIS AND that focus on the relationship between the two cultures, Carlos Fuentes's *Una familia lejana* (*Distant Relations*)[1] is the only one with a French protagonist. The greater part of the story is recounted by the Comte de Branly and then passed on to the reader by the primary narrator and co-protagonist, who turns out to be a Frenchified version of Fuentes himself. The choice of a French character as source for the bulk of the narration and of Paris as the site where the act of narrating takes place has important consequences for the novel. It establishes the center of gravity in Paris and posits Latin America as the other, regarded as such even by "Fuentes."

That the novel is a gothic romance and the fantastic is consistently associated with Latin America suggests that Latin America is doubly strange—otherworldly as well as other. Yet I cannot agree with Lanin Gyurko that *Una familia* celebrates French or European culture vis à vis this "primitive, bestial, even monstrous other."[2] Rather, I would argue that the novel problematizes any notion of a monolithic French (and, by extension, European) identity by focusing on the role Latin America plays "for" Europe and by insisting on the mixed origins of what constitutes French culture and identity.[3] The deformation of the Latin American element here—its reduction to a series of gothic *topoi*, the nightmare realm of the psyche—corresponds to what I take to be one of the main points of the novel: that the effort to deny the inevitably hybrid nature of any culture and identity leads to violent displacements. Two things will be apparent from the foregoing, namely that, as I see it, Latin America serves as a function of Europe in this novel, and, further, that its value in that relationship is both psychological and cultural, individual and collective.

In his analysis of the difference between the two cultures, Hugo Heredia contrasts the "compulsion for upheaval," which the present-day Mexican leaders inherit from the lazy, violent *encomenderos*, with the French instinct for preserving what matters to their civilization:

> You [Branly] belong to a society that does not repudiate the virtues of its ancient executioners when they become victims. Your aristocracy has been shot, guillotined, and exiled. But the political, aesthetic, and social culture of France has been zealously guarded. Thus, someone like yourself can enjoy the benefits of a vanished order along with those of the newer republican regime. (1982, 166; 160)

Una familia takes place in the Paris of the *grands boulevards*. Branly tells the greater part of his story while he and "Fuentes" are seated in the dining room of the Automobile Club of France, drinking sauterne and gazing out over the Place de la Concorde. Branly is not just a cultivated man but an aristocrat with an ancient lineage, an ancestral palace and a long life behind him. Even though this is a novel about writing novels, Fuentes avoids re-creating *la vie de bohème* that for many writers represents the quintessential Paris and that forms an integral part of Cortázar's meditation on fiction in *Rayuela*. Instead, he emphasizes the notion of a continuous and coherent civilization adhering in the values of mainstream France, those values Hugo Heredia holds up as exemplary.

Yet the historical moments to which the novel refers repeatedly, if sometimes obliquely—the Revolution; the First and Second Empires; 1870, which brought both the Prussian occupation of Paris and the Commune; and 1914—all are characterized by social upheaval, producing in the first instance the "Bonapartist opportunism" (168; 162) in France that mirrors the social confusion in Latin America during the struggle for and the early days of independence. It is clear that the continuity to which Hugo Heredia alludes is threatened by dislocation.

In fact, it has been argued that French concern with national tradition and history springs not in spite but *because* of the sense of social disorientation and the loss of continuity that mark nineteenth-century French life. In an essay on the function of social memory in postrevolutionary France, Richard Terdiman suggests that the preoccupation with the past arises, paradoxically, from the apprehension that it is no longer accessible. Recollection, which Hegel describes as "the Other made Ours—an epiphany harmonizing self and world, past and present, being and becoming," is labored. It is as a result of what Terdiman calls the "nineteenth century's memory crisis" that remembrance becomes an insistent theme in European literature (1985, 14–16).

This theme is critical to Fuentes's novel as well. It relates to the ghosts of history (personal, familial, and racial) that visit Branly and "Fuentes" and to the ghosts of literature that infiltrate the text. Especially important in this respect is the presence of Proust, which makes itself felt throughout the novel.[4] Proust's notion of involuntary memory is made explicit in the long passage in which "Fuentes" describes how certain smells, encountered in unexpected places, bring Montevideo and Buenos Aires back to him (98; 95). Proustian, too, is Branly's desire to relive his childhood. I am thinking especially of his comment that every place we visit is part of "a search for the one place we already know, a place that embraces all our emotions, all our memory" (136; 132). The taste of the madeleine restores to the Proustian protagonist his essential self, a sensation "filling me with a precious essence . . . this essence was not in me, it *was* me" (1934, 1:48). Branly's experience with the Heredias, although different in tenor, is important for the same reason: "I did not *know* the Heredias. . . . The person I came to know was myself" (136–37; 133)—a comment "Fuentes" will echo later. If anything, however, in *Una familia*, it is not the past that is recaptured but the past that recaptures. Willy-nilly, Branly and "Fuentes" are seized by and forced to recognize what they would avoid. It becomes increasingly clear that the Europeanized "Fuentes" is to be reminded of the origin he seems intent on eliding. In a sense, the entire novel is an injunction—on Branly, on "Fuentes," and on the reader as well—to remember.

Again, Fuentes's meditation on memory diverges from Proust.

For in Proust what is to be recaptured has been involuntarily lost. Fuentes sees forgetting as part of a guiltier enterprise that he relates to the very purposeful forgetting of the king's twin brother in *Le Vicomte de Bragelonne* and of Edmond Dantès in *Le Comte de Monte-Cristo*, both of whom are consigned to oblivion by those who stand to profit from their disappearance. Ultimately, the man in the iron mask seems to have been forgotten even by Dumas himself, but Dantès returns and exacts vengeance for his wrongs, visiting the sins of the fathers upon the sons. In *Una familia* as in *Terra nostra*, memory embraces all possibilities, it includes "the memory of everything that could have been and was not . . . words that were not spoken . . . opportunities that were sacrificed . . . decisions that were put off" (my translation, 1975, 566). Heredia wants to make Branly pay for his failure to help the lonely child (whose features were effaced by a metallic mask) he encountered in the Parc Monceau in his own childhood, but also for the crime his grandfather, who may have served with Maximilian in Mexico, allegedly committed upon the person of Heredia's alleged mother. His demand for recognition is an effort to rectify not just the historical record, but history itself.

Heredia's historical fantasy reminds the reader that official history is just one possible reading of events, one that is anything but disinterested.[5] For Terdiman,

> nothing is natural about our memories . . . the past—the practices, the habits, the dates and facts and places, the very furniture of our existences—is an artifice, and one susceptible of the most varied and sometimes of the most guilty manipulations. (19)

This selective process is both individual and cultural. Terdiman's interest lies in its collective dimension, the question of how a culture constructs an image of itself.[6] In the novel, Fuentes remarks on the way this process of self-editing works in Europe: "the Europeans exploited peoples of distant lands and were able, without undue effort, to forget about them" (171; 164)—just as Maximilian's soldiers conveniently forgot the blue-eyed, brown-skinned sons they left behind in Mexico (117; 114–15). Again: "we Europeans . . . quickly cast [pious veils] over our crimes against history, to enable us to accept the equally discriminatory and exigent French spirit of reason and good taste" (127; 124). This is a luxury the Latin American does not share unless he emigrates:

> We had our victims in our own homes [translation should read: at home], in ever-increasing numbers. They are the only palpable ghosts I know . . . we see them begging in the streets, sleeping on garbage heaps, daggers of glass crystallizing in their resentful gaze. (171; 164)

It is clear by the end of the novel that Hugo will meet his fate at the hands of these victims of his caste to whom he has been, at best, indifferent. For the European, as we have seen, things work differently. What happens far enough away or long enough ago is just edited out. After all, as Heredia tells Branly sarcastically, "no one has a memory that long" (117; 115).

Latin America, then, serves as a kind of bad conscience for Europe, a means of stratifying violence and classifying it as other, as alien to the traditions of European civilization. The treatment of home in Spanish American fiction that takes place in Paris tends to follow two general lines: home is seen either as a pastoral oasis happily isolated from the corrupting influences of the metropolis or as a primitive hellhole. There are significant differences between these two approaches; however, in both cases, Latin America is made to seem unreal. It becomes not a place but an idea; its history is not treated as a complex series of events with discrete causes and effects, but it is instead erased in an effort to maintain a fiction of innocence (see Blest Gana's Los trasplantados, for example) or transposed (as it is here) into a nightmare sequence that conveys the burden of collective and of individual guilt. It is the alter ego of Europe, as Fuentes argues in "La tradición literaria latinoamericana" (1988, 19).

Fuentes's interest, then—and in this he differs from Carpentier, who writes with considerable accuracy about the intrusion of French revolutionary and then imperial ambitions in Latin America—lies less in re-creating the historical moment than in exploring the psychological and cultural connection between the two continents. His attention in this novel is directed to the effect of Latin America on the French mind. The representation of Latin America and its history is filtered through the Frenchified Heredia. It is his vision that informs the image that the French

Branly transmits to "Fuentes," Frenchman manqué, who relays it with his own emendations to the reader. Not surprisingly, it follows a dream logic: events are collapsed together and become indistinguishable, dates overlap, characters are interchangeable in a logic of position that mimics the Lacanian signifying chain. Heredia's story is fragmented, full of inconsistencies and repetition. The figure of a woman playing a clavier in Branly's ornate music box becomes Mademoiselle Lange, who may or may not have been raped by Branly's father or his grandfather, who may or may not have been the Caribbean Heredia's mother, and who is also associated with the Duchesse de Langeais from Balzac's novel. The ravine into which Víctor Heredia nearly tumbles is the same ravine into which the corpse of the French woman is thrown, and also the trench that disfigures the neat lawn of the close.[7] Displacement, violence, and disruption are the norm here, and the laws of nature are suspended. Mediated by the spirit of the grotesque Heredia, Latin America becomes fantastic.

This transformation is realized in the Clos des Renards, where Branly is exposed to the other Heredia's side of the story. The close appears to be different in kind from the city of Paris, from which it remains apart. The trench that scars the garden and then simply disappears, the covered-up tarn that would normally reflect the villa, the leaves from tropical climes that fill the driveway, the dumbwaiter that leads to eternity: all suggest a setting that is allegorical rather than realistic. It serves as a kind of "theater of memory," like Giulio Camillo's invention, which is commemorated in *Terra nostra*. It is here, presided over by a Caribbean turned Frenchman, that France and Latin America meet in a surreal conjunction represented by the contrast between the "suffocating darkness of the woods" that surrounds the close and the "French park, a garden of intelligence, a chessboard" (31; 35) that leads up to the house.

In this context, the setting is to be read not as a reflection of "reality," but as a linguistic construct: "'French is like my garden, elegant,' said Heredia. 'Spanish is like my woods, indomitable'" (46; 48). Although, inevitably, Fuentes uses spacial imagery to describe the Clos, it exists only in the space created by language or art, just like the union between the goatlike André and the young Víctor, later reduced to a pair of conjoined fetuses in a kind of "journey back to the source" *à deux*.

In contrast to the Clos and to Latin America, Paris seems familiar and stable. Branly tells most of his story while he and "Fuentes" sit in the dining room of the Automobile Club, overlooking the Place de la Concorde. With its emphasis on comfort and civility, the setting is typical of the gothic romance, which almost always turns on the contrast between the cozy situation of the listener (and implicitly of the reader as well) and the chilling events that form the adventure proper. This episode takes place, as we know, not in Paris itself but in the suburbs, so that it is somehow beyond the pale, and even there the villa is hidden away in a close on the edge of a forest. Here, then, as in other gothic romances, the domain of the fantastic appears to be stowed safely out of the way of ordinary life.

But the sense of security that pervades the postprandial atmosphere of the Automobile Club is short-lived. The fantastic, which seems to be either contained in a little villa in the outskirts or relegated to the other side of the ocean, begins to spill over into Paris proper.[8] First, with the arrival of Víctor, Branly finds that his own home has been made strange, the curtains drawn and every candle lighted: "transformed by his young visitor into a forbidden, alien, distant space" (20; 25). The fact that the house is a double of another house (the Hotel Biron that houses the Rodin Museum) and that it is decorated in the almost comically ornate Empire style with which the Napoleonic nobility—ultimate winners of the revolution—tried to cover their lack of antecedents already gives some cause for uneasiness, as does the music box, a quaint bit of bric-a-brac that happens to be poisonous. During Branly's dream or trance, that familiar landmark, the Parc Monceau, appears repeatedly, peopled by ghostly figures from the past, and just before he leaves the Clos, he sees it superimposed upon the garden of the villa.

This incursion of the fantastic into Paris proper is not limited to the story within a story. The fantastic infiltrates the frame as well. Near the end of his narration, Branly's voice changes. It transmits the voices of Heredia and Clemencita and Mademoiselle Lange, which resound in the dining room, alarming his friend "Fuentes." The very act of telling the story, we learn, is an act of aggression, intended both to bring about the end of Hugo Heredia and to pass the burden of the story on to "Fuentes." After telling the story, Branly is nearly drowned by an inexplicable storm that surges up in the pool of the Automobile Club just as a waiter who may be André-Víctor passes by. A few days later, "Fuentes" visits him at home and finds that the house has, again, been made strange—with all the candles lit it recalls a Mexican church. He also finds that the ghost of Lucie, Hugo's dead wife, has installed herself as the new housekeeper while she waits for Branly to die so that she can resume life.[9]

Finally, "Fuentes" returns to the pool room of the Automobile Club of France. This spot, which is "sunk in the heart of Paris" (205; 196),[10] has become a jungle, a jungle familiar to "Fuentes" because it brings back all that he has forgotten:

> I can smell freshly cut pineapple slices, black-splotched ripe plantains, the buttery red flesh of the mamey. My mouth waters with forgotten, anticipated flavors melting on my burning tongue. . . . I walk through the bar to the swimming pool. The pool itself is obscured in a tangle of lush plants, ivy-covered trees with fragrant bark, climbing vines curling from the green mosaic pillars up to the great dome of iron and glass blinded by matted foliage. There is an overpowering aroma of venomous, ravenous flowers. Gunpowder trees: I had forgotten them. . . . My feet sink into the moist earth, the yellow mud of the edge of the swimming pool of the Automobile Club of France. Suddenly there is no sound but the chatter of the howler monkeys deep in the jungle. (224; 212–13)

The jungle, then, has taken over the very heart of Paris. The passage is presaged by an earlier one in which Heredia describes Clemencita's imaginary return to Venezuela: "I prepared a room for her here with hammocks and parrots and a small greenhouse with arcades and red tiles to deceive her" (104; 103).[11] Then, in an inversion of these scenarios, he adds, "she was the one who deceived me. She knew the New World had left its impression on Europe for all time. Don't you agree?" (105; 103). The novel demonstrates not so much the French or European presence in Latin America (this presence is the subject of *El siglo de las luces,* and it is also taken up in *El recurso del método*) as the presence of Latin America that makes itself felt in France, an echo of Frantz Fanon's argument that "Europe is literally the creation of the Third World" (1968, 102).

During Branly's narration, "Fuentes" comments,

That world, crouched in ambush, tamed only in appearances, again sprang to claw at us that last morning at the Clos des Renards, this slowly dying afternoon in the Automobile Club, as if in refutation of the prolonged calm of Cartesian reason my friend and I were struggling to save—did we truly believe that?—from the chaotic tropics of the Heredias. . . . (143; 138–39)

Demonized, the Caribbean has a will of its own and a propensity toward violence. It represents those impulses that find little space in the reasonable discourse of France, that undermine the vaunted stability and continuity of the French way. It represents the feelings, needs, and responses that are not so much alien as unacknowledged because they form no part of the nation's self-image and its collective memory, even though they erupted in French public life at those key points referred to in the novel. The Place de la Concorde, on which Branly's eyes are fixed during his narration, was earlier known as the Place de la Révolution, and it was there that the guillotine was installed. Victor Hugo uses the location to a similar effect in one of his poems, "En passant dans la place Louis XV un jour de fête publique." A forgetful crowd gathered at the Place de la Concorde dedicates itself to pleasure, while the narrator alone experiences a sense of loss. The poem serves to remind the reader of the site's bloody history and the absence it now embodies (1855, 1:409–10). The point *Una familia* makes is that the sanctification of reason, intelligence, and courtesy lends French life a sense of order that just may be factitious.

The irruption of the jungle in the heart of Paris, the appearance of the Heredias in Branly's home, the French Heredia's demand for recognition from Branly, and the return of the Count of Monte Cristo—why else does Fuentes insist on that novel?—all are variations on the theme of memory. They signify the return of the repressed, as, too, does the strange incident involving Alexander Dumas père and a black baby, whose color and provenance suggest Dumas's own origins.[12] What this confrontation with the other means ultimately for Branly and for "Fuentes" is the discovery of the self. Hence Branly's comment, "I did not know the Heredias. . . . The person I came to know was myself" (136; 133). For Branly, who is eighty-three, this recognition involves not only momentarily recapturing his youth, but even rectifying an omission committed those many years ago—the failure to hold out his hand to a lonely boy who was decidedly other, being both strange and foreign. It also includes his admission of the part that his grandfather may have played in the sordid saga of Mademoiselle Lange.

For "Fuentes," it means acknowledging the continent he has left behind. Throughout much of the narration, he passes himself off as French. He repeatedly uses the "we" and "our" forms when referring to things French and feels offended when Branly reminds him of his background, responding that "I felt more at home *here* than *there*" (155; 149). The experience of hearing Branly's story and of the events that follow it shocks him into recognition. First he admits that "at times I questioned the degree of my assimilation into the French world" (215; 204). Caught between two worlds, one he has left behind, another in which he does not quite fit, he has no home. "You do not belong here; you will never again belong there" (220; 210), says the specter of Lucie. By the end of the novel, his senses jolted by the familiar sounds and smells of the swimming pool-jungle, he is forced to admit that part of himself he has so resolutely denied: "Heredia. You are Heredia" (225; 214). But which Heredia is he: the other Mexican, who could have been his friend, or the grotesquely Francophile Carribean, who works his rude magic at the Clos des Renards?

He is both, perhaps, in a novel that explores the narrative possibilities of Borges's "The Garden of the Forking Paths." "You and I," Branly tells the narrator, "are living but one of the infinite possibilities of a life and a story" (214; 204). He then invokes another possibility: "Fuentes" returns to Mexico in 1945, instead of staying in Argentina and then moving to Paris:

> Imagine; you publish your first book of stories when you are twenty-five, your first novel four years later. You write about Mexico, about Mexicans, the wounds of a body, the persistence of a few dreams, the masks of progress. You remain forever identified with that country and its people. (215; 204–5)

Imagine, in other words—since it is not stated here—that you are Fuentes without quotation marks. If the author's life represents an unrealized alternative for the narrator, the narrator's life and the novel itself represent the same for Fuentes, a way of exploring the consequences of a choice he did not make, since, in fact, he did return to Mexico after living in Buenos Aires, and he did become the "hypothetical" novelist Branly describes.

I am not suggesting that the author has been immune to the temptation of Paris. He wrote *Una familia* at a point when he had been living much in the French capital (1965–66, 1968, 1972, 1975–77). The conversations he enjoyed with Paul Morand at the swimming pool of the Royal Automobile Club served as the basis for the lengthy talk that comprises the greater part of the novel, and Morand himself, author of *Paris galant*, was the model for Branly (Fuentes 1980, 69–70). I suspect finally that by including a version of himself in the novel Fuentes could examine the fascination that French life and literature have exerted on his life as well as on the lives of so many other Latin American writers.

The shadowy presence of the real Fuentes in the novel represents the possibility of a synthesis uniting cultures and times. The novel's ending suggests what happens when the other is denied: the revenge of a past that has been elided, as it has with "Fuentes," with Branly, and with Hugo Heredia. There is, after all, no redemption for the executioner-victims of the Count of Monte Cristo. And Branly suggests as another possibility that the novel may have already been written—"Its author, need I say it? is Alexandre Dumas" (216; 205). *Una familia* is filled with references to reflecting pools. They offer a means of self-revelation more dangerous than the mirrors that also abound here. The last line of the madrigal of "La claire fontaine" comes to Branly only in his final scene: "j'ai trouvé l'eau si belle, que je m'y suis noyé" (I found the water so beautiful that I drowned, 209; 199).

Since self-discovery here involves the realization of one's connection to, or even identity with, the other, it may devolve into a more radical form of alienation than any suffered before: dispossession of soul. Yet it is his specter that leads "Fuentes" to a realization critical to this very literary novel. He becomes aware of the presence of important Latin American writers who have lived and worked in Paris:

I know that . . . from that bridge, at the very moment Nerval was writing *El desdichado*, César Vallejo was gazing at his reflection in the rushing waters; on the Boulevard La Tour-Maubourg I will hear the voice of Pablo Neruda; on the Rue de Longchamp, that of Octavio Paz. . . . (222; 211)

The novel ends on an ambiguous note. Will "Fuentes" lose all by becoming Heredia, or will he become a more complete man in touch with his racial and personal past, perhaps a Mexican novelist living in Paris? Will he perhaps become Fuentes? There is no single answer. After all, "No one remembers the whole story" (225; 214).

The outcome, Fuentes insists, depends on the reader's interpretation, "on his capacity to assume the story, to continue it and to pass it on to someone else" (my translation, 1989, 647); there is no "right" reading and, for that reason, no final outcome: "the novel never ends. The narration has to be passed on to other hands immediately; that's its destiny" (1989, 643).

Una familia not only opens itself to further interpretation, but it is also a reading—or readings—of earlier texts. In this sense it does provide a model for dealing with ghosts of the past—the ghosts of literature. We have already referred to Proust, Dumas, and Carpentier. Equally important here are the French writers who came from Latin America: Jules Supervielle, Jules Laforgue, Isidore Ducasse, and José María de Heredia. (Fuentes appropriates the latter's name because it evokes the theme of the transatlantic double: the French writer's cousin, José María Heredia without the "de," lived in America and wrote his poetry in Spanish.) If these ghosts cannot be exorcised, they can be incorporated harmoniously into the text, affording the kind of dialogue with the past (and with other cultures) that Bakhtin calls a "memory model" because it is, in Terdiman's words, "not a dispossession but a liberating recollection of the collective condition of language" (1985, 23). The text itself stands as a model of cultural diversity.

Of these ghosts of Latin American beginnings, Supervielle is especially important. His poem, "La chambre voisine," cited in its entirety in the novel, provides a kind of rudimentary plot structure.[13] It ties in with the notion of an adjacent reality or irreality—another continent, another culture, another life, the phantom self or double—on which Fuentes's novel is based. Supervielle was the only one of these writers to return to Latin

America, which he did frequently, managing, perhaps, in this way to reconcile the two cultures within his own life, as presumably Fuentes, too, has done. The narrator commends Supervielle for the happy synthesis he reaches within the poem, allowing readers to approach

> [the] French spirit of reason and good taste, but not to sacrifice the cutting edge of the fantasy, the displacement, the revelatory madness, of the vast, empty lands of the new continent. (127; 124).

Fuentes draws our attention to these models of transcultural creativity. But, oddly enough, he hides another model in plain sight: Luis Buñuel, to whom *Una familia* is dedicated and whose work in French, Mexican, and Spanish cinema makes him a model of cultural diversity.

The recurrence of images and turns of phrase from a 1970 article on Buñuel's work suggests that Fuentes may have looked it over again when he was writing the novel, and it also serves to alert the reader to clues about Buñuel's presence. For Fuentes, the scene in *Le Chien andalou* where a woman's eye is sectioned by a razor provides a key to Buñuel's films; all involve

> a struggle of conflicting visions . . . the impure, desiring, revolutionary eyes of the totality, opposed to the blindness of the established order. (My translation, 1970, 198)

The violence of Buñuel's films, then, serves to open our eyes to "everything that [the established order] has hidden, mutilated, disfigured or stripped of its name, its place or its reflection" (208). It serves to put us in touch with the greater reality, to introduce a different perception, or, to phrase the same idea differently—and this is a central tenet of surrealism—to unite the opposites in "in an uneasy and unnerving synthesis" (213) that is never quite achieved, never abandoned.

The violence in *Una familia*, too, is intended to make both characters and readers aware of a larger world, to see what is normally off limits. The trench is "a long, deep scar, a knife slash through this rational and most perfect of gardens" (74; 75), much like the sectioned eye of *Le chien*. The loutish Heredia, who vacillates between Heapish servility and outright rudeness, will call into question the comfortable order of French life, disrupting Branly's genteel existence. Just so, the unlikely Branly will later perform his own acts of aggression, forcing "Fuentes" to confront the world he would leave behind and delivering Hugo Heredia over to the "palpable ghosts" (171; 164) he has overlooked at home. They are the same ghosts Fuentes describes in his essay on Buñuel: "the ghosts in Buñuel's films are the impoverished children from Las Hurdes and the criminal children from the slums of Mexico" (207).

Part of that violence against the established order in Buñuel's films and here as well is directed against established narrative conventions. Fuentes has said that his working method in *Una familia* was inspired by Buñuel's account of the way he and Dalí wrote *Le Chien andalou*. They made an effort to avoid all the logical connections involved in the "well-made" story and consciously opened themselves to that "edge of fantasy" Fuentes admires (1982, 124; for Buñuel's account, see *Mi último suspiro*, 1982, 124–25). In his later films, particularly *Belle de Jour* (1967) and *Le Charme discret de la bourgeoisie* (1972), Buñuel again takes up his attack on narrative convention by contaminating the frame with the dream and introducing dreams within dreams so that the dividing line between fantasy and reality becomes hopelessly muddled. Fuentes puts these techniques to good effect, as we have seen, in this tribute to his old friend. The undermining of narrative certainty and the ambiguity of the ending have the same purpose in the novel as in Buñuel's films: "restoring responsibility to its origin: to each spectator's conscience and imagination" (213).[14]

For all its playfulness and melodrama, *Una familia* turns on an ethical issue: the need to recognize and acknowledge the other. It contests an essentialist notion of culture by showing that the denial of a culture's (or an individual's) inevitably hybrid nature leads to deformation, dislocation, and violence. Fuentes's insistence on the contribution made by writers of Latin American origin to French literature also shows that the interaction of different cultures need not be destructive. The point Fuentes makes is that we must learn to think of cultures, in James L. Clifford's words, "not as organically unified or traditionally continuous but rather as negotiated present processes" (1988, 213) that will be enriched instead of diminished by the admission of foreign elements.

In the passage from the novel involving the commemoration of Latin American writers working in Paris, one thing is clear. Paris, site of the narration, is the enabling space that allows writers to write, whatever their nationality is or wherever they find their material. And this is true, in large part, because it accepts foreigners into its Bohemia, if not into its official culture. The images of the world of fantasy overtaking the heart of the city, then, also depict the process of creation.

And yet it is somehow troubling that throughout *Una familia* Fuentes sees Latin America with the European eye. It is always the other, always exotic, like Proust's description of Gustave Moreau's strange scenes, with which it is associated here: "venemous flowers interwoven with precious jewels" (12; 17). Paris, no matter how threatened by incursions of the exotic and the imaginative, remains the center of gravity of this text, itself written in Paris. The city is the constant frame of reference of the narrative; it is the present. Even if it were toppled, it would leave solid ruins. But Latin America in this novel has no solidity. It is reduced to a dream world, a confluence of emotions, a memory, an idea, the guilty conscience, or the suppressed emotions of France. In *Una familia*, Latin America is always "la chambre voisine."

6

No Man's Land:
Reencuentro de personajes

REENCUENTRO DE PERSONAJES (REUNION OF CHARACTERS)[1] INVOLVES A
cast of Mexican expatriates whose sense of self is based on their
having met F. Scott Fitzgerald years ago and their conviction that
he has described them in *Tender Is the Night* and that they also
served as models for characters in Evelyn Waugh's *Brideshead
Revisited*. The protagonist of *Reencuentro*, a young Mexican
woman modeled on Elena Garro herself, has left her husband for
one of this group, "a savage dressed like an Englishman" (42),
who uses her as a cover for his homosexual liaisons and as an
object of humiliation. The plot turns on Verónica's attempt to
decipher who, or what, Frank is and, through him, who or what
she is herself. Central to the novel is the question of identity—
cultural, sexual, personal, and literary—and the related question
of authority. These matters are especially problematic in a text
that frames other texts and that is further complicated by Garro's
hidden agenda. In addition to *Tender Is the Night* and *Brideshead Revisited*, another intertext is incorporated covertly and
parodically in the novel: *El laberinto de la soledad* (*The Labyrinth of Solitude*), Octavio Paz's exploration of the Mexican psyche. Further, the novel hints that the reader should look beyond
literature to life, specifically Garro's failed marriage to Paz. The
title, with its emphasis on self-conscious fictionality, is disingenuous. The mystery of Frank's identity, based on a complex
interplay between texts, is solved not in the works of Fitzgerald
or Waugh but in the character of Paz himself.

Riven from context, the earlier texts are refocused from a marginal perspective. Here secondary characters of exotic origin
loom large, while the protagonists virtually disappear. The origi-

nals are inevitably distorted by being transposed to a different context. In her book on parody, Linda Hutcheon argues that a work can be parodic without including ridicule and without being comic. What is essential is the ironic inversion of an earlier text. She cites as an example Euripides' *Medea*, long considered to be a parody of Sophocles and Aeschylus because the hero was replaced with a protagonist who is both a woman and an outsider (1985, 6). In this sense, Garro's treatment of the Fitzgerald and Waugh novels is parodic (and it is in this sense that I shall be using the term here). She is not, however, interested in writing an extended parody of these works; instead, she uses them as points of departure for a very different novel.

The game of literary doubles is fairly complicated. Briefly, Garro identifies Frank with Francisco, "the Queen of Chile," a character who makes a brief appearance in *Tender Is the Night*. The scene is cited in full in *Reencuentro*. The young man's father asks Dick Diver to use his skill as a psychoanalyst in order to cure the son's homosexuality. Diver interviews Francisco, but he soon determines that the young man does not want to be cured and so refuses to take the case. Garro identifies Eddy with Luis Campion, a lachrymose fellow who appears more frequently in the novel. Fitzgerald uses both Campion and Francisco to point up his theme of moral decay. According to Garro's novel, Fitzgerald met their prototypes while he was staying in Lausanne at a time when Zelda was under treatment at a nearby psychiatric clinic. If such a meeting did take place, it would have been in 1930–31. But there is no reference in the Fitzgerald literature to the author's having any definite models in mind for Francisco and Campion. Garro claims in an interview that she herself met these people in Paris around 1961, but she does not mention names.[2]

As for *Brideshead Revisited*, Garro argues that Frank, who sometimes uses the alias Arturo F. Bartlett, served Waugh as the model for Anthony Blanche. He is an Argentine Jew, educated at Eton, who is "the 'aesthete' *par excellence*, a byword of iniquity" (Garro cites *BR* in translation, 260; Waugh 1945, 32). Blanche contributes to the downfall of Sebastian, an innocent figure connected in *Reencuentro* with Mikel, who was seduced and abandoned by Frank many years before and whose fate and appearance are repeated in Verónica. Most authorities agree that

Waugh's portrait of Anthony Blanche was based primarily on his good friend Harold Acton—much to Acton's dismay—with a few traces of Brian Howard (see the discussion in *The Diaries of Evelyn Waugh* 1976, 791, 797). In Verónica's judgment, "Fitzgerald did not understand Frank, he considered him banal and insignificant; he failed to see the evil lurking in that youngster" (261). It is Waugh, she believes, who understood Frank's potential for evil. In *Brideshead*, then, Garro seizes on Blanche's cruelty and his air of viciousness and, of course, his cosmopolitan background. Waugh's narrator describes him as an Englishman manqué, who has not had the kind of childhood that allows successful Englishmen to work off the savage side (46–47). Garro chooses to overlook both the comic elements in Waugh's portrayal and his insistence on Blanche's great intelligence.

Garro cannibalizes both *Brideshead Revisited* and *Tender Is the Night* to make a satiric point about a certain kind of Latin American, the kind that looks to European models for definition. Together the two novels exercise an almost biblical authority over the characters in *Reencuentro*, who find in them a culture to be emulated and keys for understanding their destiny: hence the extensive, reverent use of quotation. The parodic elevation of both works to sacred texts of Western culture points to a concern that Garro broaches in an interview. She argues that there is a close link between a sense of national identity and the great works of fiction:

> the writer provides us with a pattern. Homer invented the Greeks. After Homer, the Greeks were all alike; they were all Achilles. Cervantes invented the Spaniards. After Cervantes, they were either Sancho Panza or Don Quixote. O'Neill invented the Americans. Scott Fitzgerald invented the modern age. But the Mexicans. . . . The genius who will tell us what we are like, or what we should be like, has yet to be born. (1978, 215)[3]

Lacking this model, Garro's characters are forced into an absurd dependence on the foreign text.

Garro, then, treats questions of origin, legitimacy, and authority here as functions of the written word. In *Reencuentro* we are faced with characters whose sense of self has been fixed by the literature of other peoples. Hence come Frank's insistence on speaking English, wearing English suits and inventing friendships with people like the Duke and Duchess of Windsor, and the tenacity with which everyone in his group clings to the memory of their brief meeting with Scott Fitzgerald. By claiming a stake in the novels that define the modern period, they hope to arrogate for themselves some portion of the authority, the legitimacy, reserved for the elect of the time—the North Americans (and to a lesser degree the English), triumphant expatriates who claimed Paris as their own during the Jazz Age. The Latin Americans were distinctly eccentric, in both senses of the word—Anthony Blanche's absurd affectations, Francisco's nickname ("The Queen of Chile"), and Campion's penchant for public displays of weeping come to mind. Dependent on foreign sources for definition and fixated on an earlier period, Garro's characters are a congery of pretensions and gestures enclosing a void. They are not *personas* (people) but *personajes* (characters), as the title suggests, reduced to repeating the secondary roles that are meted out to them. Watching them gathered together, Verónica reflects that

> There was something ghostly about that gathering, something artificial, as if each of the guests were playing a role that had been played long before by the real protagonists of some drama that Verónica had not seen, but that she knew about from the literature, the films and the newspapers of the twenties. . . . (213)

Finally, she concludes that they are all impostors.

This effort on the part of the characters to appropriate an identity, to assert their right to a position in the center rather than the periphery of an ethnocentric world—in other words, to affirm their legitimacy in terms of society—is underlined by the question of personal legitimacy. Paz argues that "the question of origin is the secret center of our anxiety and anguish" (my translation, 1959, 72). Both Frank's and Eddy's mothers are notorious for their affairs, and Eddy argues that "all of us South Americans are made of the same clay. His mother was an old whore and his father an old cuckold" (216). Frank has his father certified. The act of usurpation allows him to feel secure about his origin—he is, imaginatively at least, self-engendered. This act also makes it possible for him to assume the father's authority, which in the Oedipal scheme is absolute. Even more brutal in his search for social legitimacy, Frank resorts to illicit, not to say antisocial, means. He murders Logan, the rich North American whose fortune he and his partner (Logan's new wife, Cora) will share, and later he murders at least two other people who threaten to expose him.

Frank and Cora are both mestizos literally and figuratively. They are caught between the world of high civilization, represented by Paris and the English public schools, and an archaic world in which violence offers a natural solution to difficulties: "Some quality that was centuries old made Frank act like a savage and left him in possession of a universe unlike Verónica's, a universe where dark things happened, things that had been forgotten a long time ago" (41–42). The key to Frank's character is not really to be found in Fitzgerald and Waugh. Rather it is furnished by a text never mentioned in the novel—*El laberinto de la soledad*, a book that sets out to do what Garro denied had been done for the Mexicans: to tell them who they are.

In *El laberinto*, Paz describes the Mexican man as isolated, hermetic, hidden, his relationship with the outside world governed by his concept of life as "a chance to fuck someone over or to be fucked over. That is, to humiliate, punish and hurt. Or the other way around" (my translation, 1959, 71). Frank is a parodic version of Paz's Mexican. He, too, is a loner: "He moved in an isolated world, and wherever he went, absolute solitude was produced" (94). He is hidden—he lies, uses different names, assumes different attitudes, pretends to be dead—and a real manipulator. Having failed in his attempt to form a new identity based on foreign cultural models (Frank never really cuts the mustard in Europe), he simply moves on to another role, asserting his manliness over the vulnerable. Homosexual himself—and this tendency, of course, is a logical extension of machismo—he picks as targets the passive homosexuals for whom, according to Paz, the Mexican reserves his scorn (71), and Verónica, who becomes a social outcast when she leaves her husband. By humiliating Verónica, who looks English and is socially adept, Frank manages to revenge himself, however obliquely, on the culture that has rejected him.

Yet for all her sophistication, Verónica, too, believes in a world divided along lines of authority and obedience. For her, the concept is idealized in the relationship between father and daughter.

As she sees it, her unhappiness is the direct result of filial disobedience: "Her first mistake had been to disobey her father by
marrying without his consent; after that the deluge had fallen,
and she had been seized by terror" (29). Like all adults, Verónica
must now live, irremediably, in the fallen world, but for her there
is no notion of *felix culpa*. Instead, she longs for an impossible
return to childhood: "If she could go back home and forget that
she had ever tried to go out into the world, then she would
no longer be terrified" (202). The paternal home continues to
represent for her an ideal of stability and order:

> When she was a child, in her childhood home, words and bread and
> the way people looked at you or moved had an exact place and their
> effects were as enduring as Fra Angelico's colors, or Ghiberti's Gates
> of Paradise or Mozart's music. Now she had no home, her brothers
> and sisters were scattered among strange in-laws, her family had
> been overtaken by the jungle. (43)

In his discussion of the radical solitude in which the Mexican
lives, Paz comments that in some cases, among them those involving separation from the parents, "being alone is identified
with being orphaned, and both conditions are expressed in a
sense of sin" (my translation, 1959, 58). Whereas some races may
transcend the loneliness and the shame that accompanies this
consciousness of separation, he argues, the Mexican remains
closed up within the self (58).

For Verónica there is no question of redemption. She sub-
scribes to an Old Testament morality that accords well with the
Mexican popular story about the little girl who is transformed
into a monster because she disobeyed her parents. Convinced of
her essential guiltiness and terrified of new punishment, Verónica readily accedes to the demands of Frank, who is much older,
calls her "little girl," keeps her in a state of total dependence,
and punishes her for her transgressions.

Eddy says, "Children should be taught to disobey; that's the
only way they can get away from people as evil as Cora and
Frank" (214). Verónica's idealization of childhood and her habit
of obedience make her an easy prey for these exacting step-
parents. Rather than an *inversion*, the drama played out in the
stark Paris flat is a *stripped-down version* of the play enacted at

home. The relationship between Verónica and Frank lays bare the structure of control, which in the familial relationship is naturalized. The furnished apartment Verónica and Frank rent in Paris is a heartless version of the paternal home:

> The fireplaces made of white marble were empty, the chairs and sofas covered in silk were uninviting. . . . The flat had high ceilings and white walls. The only thing Verónica remembered about it was the cold wind that came through the curtains and blew over the canopy bed. The apartment was oppressive. "There's an evil spell here," she told herself. . . . (94–95)

Upstairs, the landlord's quarters are decorated with erotic objects that proclaim his interest in necrophilia. Verónica notices in particular a doll that hangs inside a black cage. Later she associates Frank's lovemaking with the landlord's necrophilia and her own fate with the doll's (104). She notes that in Frank's hands, "she became an object and the act of love, an erotic technique" (94)—a natural outcome of a view that reduces the world to a place where you use or get used. The home, then, which should provide protection, itself becomes a source of danger, a prison instead of a shelter, where the act of love is associated only with death.

The city is an extension of the apartment. Garro shows interest in representing neither the dense life nor the monuments of Paris. Although the characters talk constantly of Fitzgerald and Waugh, no street scene brings a passage to mind. There are no street scenes. Except for a network of spies and accomplices, the city seems emptied out, depopulated, an absence rather than a presence. Verónica is occasionally reminded of its beauty, but it remains inaccessible. Instead, she faces a nightmarish landscape in which "vampires" (138) "circulate at night" (133). For Véronica, it is coterminous with adulthood, the post-Edenic world she identifies with her sense of terror (see 29 and 202). Ironically, for all that Paris represents in terms of the social validation so dear to the heart of the Mexicans as they are rendered both in this novel and in El laberinto de la soledad, the city lacks substance here. It is a blank screen against which primitive struggles are projected, a place where the darker forces are loosed under the cover of anonymity.[4] Having failed in his attempt to penetrate "the center of society" (193–94), Frank takes advantage of his marginality. In Mexico, where he is known, he is careful about observing the social norms (even his elopement with Verónica is a sanctioned part of male behavior). But in Paris he gives free rein to his impulses. The city serves as an open field in which to practice the very Mexican sport of doing to others before they can do to you (Paz 1959, 71).

Finally, like many Latin Americans whose social expectations are frustrated, Frank returns home. There his display of European culture and North American wealth command respect. His life has followed a trajectory similar to his mother's, who begins by imitating all that is English and winds up in her old age embracing a reified image of the Mexican: Dolores del Río (82). In Mexico, where he lives with his mother, his wife, and his four children, Frank enjoys the authority of the lord and master: "He had achieved status as he grew old, living at home in Mexico, surrounded by luxury and regarded with respect" (249). Verónica stays on in Paris, a victim more of her own fear than of Frank. She endlessly rereads *Tender Is the Night* and *Brideshead Revisited* because she is convinced that her destiny is inscribed in the pages of those novels. For her the city is a prison.

As I suggested earlier, Fitzgerald's and Waugh's works function here as the sacred texts of Western culture; they represent the Word and, as such, serve the characters as both a model for behavior and a source of revelation. Viewed as reenactment, the characters' lives seem to be already written, therefore predestined, and their identities subsumed in the rôle—hence the title. But these works are inevitably distorted in the translation as they are put to uses that the authors surely never envisaged. Further, the two novels are infiltrated covertly by a third text—*El laberinto de la soledad*. As a result, Anthony Blanche/Frank is found conspiring with a beautiful mestiza to murder a rich North American and assure his own place in the beau monde. And Fitzgerald is chided for missing the mark in his portrayal of Francisco, the "Queen of Chile," because he did not understand "Frank." Like much parody, *Rencuentro de personajes* sets out to amend the earlier works, supplementing here what it sees as inadequate. Finally, the novel—juncture of these three texts—remits the informed reader to a fourth source—Garro's version of her failed marriage to Paz.

Although she never openly alludes to the marriage, she does provide clues suggesting that for her portrait of Frank she drew not only on *El laberinto de la soledad* but also on its author. She and Paz were married, in a ceremony of dubious legality, in 1937. In 1945, they moved to Paris, where, like Frank and Verónica, they took an apartment on the Avenue Victor Hugo. Her comments show that she felt herself victimized by a Paz whom she saw as high-handed and prone to giving orders while she herself was only too obedient (1979, 41 and elsewhere). In the nonfictional *Memorias de España 1937*, published in 1992, she compares her marriage to life in "a boarding school with strict rules and constant scolding" (my translation, 150). *Reencuentro*, like *Testimonios sobre Mariana*, which also involves characters modeled on Garro and her ex-husband, was written before she left Paris in 1964 but after Paz had deserted her and married again (1986, 69). In *Testimonios*, the husband is cruel and notoriously unfaithful, but not criminal. These are highly imaginative renditions of a marriage gone sour. Just to what extent they correspond to the reality is unclear since there is as yet no biography of either spouse.

At the end of *Reencuentro de personajes*, Verónica is left alone in Paris, still controlled at a distance by Frank and too fearful to go to the police with the notebook that would reveal his crimes. Although Garro did not get stuck in Paris—she has traveled widely since the days of her marriage—she, too, was fearful of publishing the novel in which she would expose the "real" Paz (I am speaking, of course, of the version of Paz adumbrated here). As she told Joseph Sommers in a 1965 interview, "It's terrible, and I don't dare publish it" (my translation, 1978, 217). She did not do so until almost twenty years after she wrote it.

In writing and ultimately, if belatedly, publishing the work, Garro stakes out her own claim to authority. But she does so obliquely, hiding behind Fitzgerald and Waugh, structuring her account of the relationship as a crime story, as indeed she may have seen it. One of her goals apparently was to defame Paz in such a way that he would be unable to defend himself. The novel *hints* that the key to Frank's identity involves Garro's ex-husband. However, it *states* that the solution to this enigma is to be found in *Tender Is the Night* and *Brideshead Revisited*. In his review of *Testimonios sobre Mariana*, Daniel Balderston discusses the

deployment of gossip as a narrative strategy: "it attacks by drawing close to the realm of real life, and defends itself by taking
refuge in the realm of the imagination" (my translation, 1983,
115). What makes it so effective, he suggests, is the ease with
which it moves from one world to another. This use of gossip
accords beautifully with the requirements for revenge: that the
offender recognize that vengeance is being taken and that the
avenger escape punishment for the revenge.

The intricate play between texts that marks the novel is, then,
in part a cover-up. But it also points to a legitimate concern with
the problem of Latin American identity—specifically, the sense
that Latin Americans are the creation of other, more powerful,
cultures, that they are, to quote Paz, who is summarizing Leo-
poldo Zea, "thought up by other people" (my translation, 1959,
152). Garro uses parody here to a satiric end: to expose both the
Anglo-American arrogance of attitude toward what they would
consider "Wogs" and the inferiority complex that led many Latin
Americans to share this attitude. She takes the idea seriously but
treats it playfully. How else can we explain why her characters
conceive of the absurd notion that their destiny has been written
by Scott Fitzgerald and Evelyn Waugh and that they are stuck
with the minor roles assigned to them?

But, like Ribeyro in La juventud en la otra ribera, Garro also
explores a countermovement that reverses the direction of the
Conquest. It is the exploitation of Europe, particularly Paris, by
picaros like Frank who acquire the cultural trappings and the
wealth there that will enable them to retire to the good life at
home, much as the indianos once did after making their fortunes
in America. If Paris had at one point become synonymous with
self-fulfillment and freedom, a kind of utopia of the spirit, it
takes on here the more material guise of an El Dorado open to
plunder. Verónica calls it "the hopeless city; when there's nothing left to be done, desperate people always head for Paris" (84–
85). Like the American wilderness, it is populated by the castoffs
of other societies. The only French character in the novel is the
maid, Yvette; the others are Latin American, East European, and
Turkish. For Verónica, it is a penal colony where she is condemned to harsh labor in the modern Parisian equivalent of the
mine: the boutique.[5]

This exploitation and inversion of cultural expectations is reflected at the level of the text by Garro's blatant appropriation of the earlier novels. In *Reencuentro*, as we have seen, they become part of something quite different. Oswald de Andrade describes this process of active textual and cultural consumption as "*anthropophagy* . . . a critical devouring of the European contribution, and its transformation into a new product" (paraphrased in Campos 1980, 231). Although Garro does not openly attack Fitzgerald's and Waugh's texts, her focus on the marginal and the exceptional conveys an implicit criticism of their ethnocentric view of the Latin American.

Garro supplements this inadequate view with types borrowed from *El laberinto de la soledad*, portrait of the Mexican written by a Mexican. But this work, too, is undercut in *Reencuentro*. Garro exaggerates—and consequently ironizes—Paz's ideas, presenting the archetypal Mexican as a homosexual thug with a veneer of culture and a history of crime, and his consort as a victim who is terrified that her lover will murder her. Recast as melodrama and focused from the perspective of the woman, Paz's text is destabilized, and he himself is accused of the related phenomena that he analyzes: imitation and machismo.

Garro parodies Paz's text here with a double intent. She mounts a ferocious *argumentum ad hominem*, but she also explores the effects of the patriarchal system on an intelligent and cultivated woman. She is very aware of the sexual analog of literary and cultural colonialism. The protagonist of *Reencuentro* is a woman whose part has been assigned her (in other words, who has been thought up) by others—her father (who has cast her out for disobedience), her husband (whom she flees), Frank, Fitzgerald, Waugh, and, indirectly, Paz. The sense of terror infusing the novel comes not so much from Verónica's exile in the adult world as from her being helplessly caught in a plot that she does not quite understand. (Both meanings of the word "plot" are relevant here.) Verónica dares not edit the text, only interpret it. Trapped in this role by the cultural forces that created her, she is in a very literal sense the female reader to whom Cortázar derisively refers in *Rayuela* (1966, 398; 1987, 454).

Yet curiously enough, although parodying it, Garro does not reject Paz's concept of Mexican identity. Indeed, her experience must have authenticated that vision of a society in which the strong exercise an unwritten right to prey on the weak. Yet her outrage is directed not so much against the system as against the allocation of power. The novel is a plea not for a more humane approach to human relations but for a shift in power. Verónica's response to Frank's cruelty is the reiterated threat that she will make him pay for what he has done, a promise she cannot make good. In Reencuentro, only Garro is the final source of authority, arrogating for herself the say-so that escaped her in the marriage as it does her helpless surrogate, who reads her fate in the works of others. Garro claims the authority of the victim, of one who has suffered and learned from real experience. The appeal to life authenticates her position; it is through the text that she asserts it, and she intends to have an influence that goes beyond the literary. The transformation from victim to author—someone who wields authority in the text—by means of the pen suggests a parallel sexual transformation from "fuckee" to "fucker." The novel is brilliantly calculated to humiliate her ex-husband. In doing so, Garro demonstrates, quite unconsciously I suspect, the concept of Mexican identity that Paz both decries and, according to her, embodies: the vision of life as "a chance to fuck someone over or to be fucked over."

7

Paris Is Burning:
Paisajes después de la batalla

JUAN GOYTISOLO'S *PAISAJES DESPUÉS DE LA BATALLA (LANDSCAPES After the Battle)*[1] is set entirely in Paris, a Paris that is just a shadow of its former self. Here, the city is not the greatest capital of all, as Carrillo saw it, but a displaced-persons camp (as in the Andrzej Wajda film for which it is named), threatened by masses of exiles who are about to engulf the boulevards and claim that terrain as their own. It is the capital of the third world now rather than the first, which is represented by an invasion of North American products and advertising techniques. Both an examination and a projection, the novel belongs to that line of postmodern literature that envisages, almost optimistically, the destruction of the city (Pike 1981, 118).[2] In *Paisajes*, the protagonist-author quite literally deconstructs Paris, reducing its monuments, physical and spiritual, to rubble. Near the end, the city lies in ruins, its fallen stones overgrown with weeds and vines, as the protagonist waits for the time bomb fastened to his chest to explode and leave him, too, in a shattered state.

The chief intent of *Paisajes*, as I read it, is the desacralization of Western culture, represented by monumental Paris. The novel represents an indictment of Western political ideas, literature, and society, especially late-twentieth-century consumer society. Goytisolo's focus on the non-Western, immigrant population living in the Sentier has a satiric effect similar to that gained in earlier literature by having an uncontaminated savage visit so-called civilization.[3] It calls into question whether modernity need be the goal of all cultural development.[4] The novel is headed by an epigraph from *Bouvard et Pécuchet*, Flaubert's encyclopedic send-up of nineteenth-century bourgeois life. It describes itself as, among other things, an epic poem (103; 128), a compilation of all human knowledge (153; 188), "a lesson on things territories History" (157; 193), and "a meticulous exposé of the clichés of the period" (149; 184).[5] The protagonist's researches into contemporary life parallel Bouvard and Pécuchet's forays into the branches of human knowledge, and the results are equally deflationary.

In his effort to expose the assumptions of contemporary society in the West, Goytisolo draws on many and varied sources. All are important to the book's encyclopedic dimension and also to the notion of city experience, but he draws most heavily on the storehouse of cultural and mass cultural cliché. He "deideologizes" (Achille Bonito-Oliva's term, quoted in Jameson 1991, 324) high culture and politics by representing them through the techniques of mass culture. And he simultaneously turns mass culture against itself by isolating its representations from their normal context. Finally, he holds up the trajectory of his protagonist and alter ego, the fictive Goytisolo, as an exemplum of both the cultural tolerance he advocates for society and the marginalization he believes is essential to the disinterested intellectual (149; 183–84). This biographical development (temporal) is paralleled spatially by the shift in focus in the novel from monumental Paris to the Sentier.

The process of deideologization central to *Paisajes* is effected principally through its emphasis on the multiethnic dimension of urban experience and on the marginal nature of the narrator-protagonist. Heterogeneous materials are incorporated, including especially the parodic appropriation of the clichés (both form and substance) of advanced industrial society. In the following pages, I shall examine these factors in some detail. They have important consequences for representation in the novel, notably for the image Goytisolo presents here of late-twentieth-century Paris and of the protagonist, whose biography mirrors and is mirrored by the city.

The hecatomb with which the novel opens proclaims Goytisolo's intention of sacrificing the familiar elements of the city. It also signals that the change will be effected through language— the "texte de la ville" (street and shop signs, grafitti, even snatches of conversation; Butor 1985, 71), the protagonist's patchwork narration, the novel itself. With the overnight transformation of all public signs into Arabic (acceleration of a process already under way), the native Parisians are thrown into consternation, strangers in their own home. Their shared consciousness is ruptured by the intrusion of foreign elements that produce a polyphonic discourse—"the babelization of great cities" (my translation, Goytisolo quoted in García Gabaldón, 1988, 53)—just as the smug tone of the "we" narrator (itself a product of nineteenth-century realism) is interrupted repeatedly by the tergiversations of the eccentric protagonist/narrator. This disappropriation of the French is accompanied by a displacement of the locus of value in the novel from the West to the third world and the locus of the narration from the customary haunts of fiction (the boulevards, the Latin Quarter) to the Sentier, a district with a big immigrant population (including the author himself).

In situating the novel in the Sentier, Goytisolo explicitly rebuffs the expectations of readers. His protagonist, the narrator tells us, avoids "the elegant, refined, artistic milieux that so fascinate the novelistic heroes of Carpentier or Cortázar." He will never be seen riding in a horse-drawn carriage down "one of the splendid avenues that converge at the Etoile, in the company of Reynaldo Hahn or some other intimate of the Verdurin clan," as does the Prime Minister in *El recurso del método*. Instead, he frequents "spaces with no literary past whatsoever" (85; 107–8). Goytisolo uses stock literary notions about Paris as a screen against which he can project his own vision of the city, repeatedly contrasting what he sees as the monolithic culture of the boulevards with the cultural relativism of the Sentier. In the Sentier:

> The antlike hustle and bustle of the street, its creative vegetable luxuriance offer him each day a continuous, free variety show. . . . The gradual de-Europeanization of the city—the appearance of Oriental souks and hammams, peddlers of African totems and necklaces, graffiti in Arabic and Turkish—fills him with rejoicing. The complexity of the urban environment—that dense and ever-changing territory irreducible to logic and to programming—invites him on every hand to ever-shifting itineraries. . . . (85–86; 108)

As the passage makes clear, Goytisolo undercuts one myth in order to put a fresher one in its place. Although he makes a point of its aliterary nature, he uses the Sentier much in the way the

surrealists used the arcades or Cortázar used the Latin Quarter—
that is, to supply a sense of mystery and depth, a potential for
adventure, that the modern city seems otherwise to lack. In this
schema, a half-hidden vista, an odd repetition, a fortuitous encounter all hold out a promise of meaning for the person who
knows how to read the city. And so Goytisolo writes that "the
walls of the buildings of Le Sentier, the white-tiled corridors of
the métro, offer all sorts of invitations and solicitations to anyone
who wishes or knows how to read them" (29; 42). To go out
into the streets of the Sentier, where "the basements and attics
abandoned by the indigenous residents harbor mysterious ritual
festivities" (133–34; 165), is to receive "a mysterious lesson in
topography" (86; l08), to "tame new territories" (29; 42). The
Sentier is the space that allows Goytisolo the necessary play of
imagination to write, a space he has himself created and that he
shares with his protagonist, the other Goytisolo, "his territory,
his turf" (134; 165).

In this idealized vision of the Sentier, Goytisolo conflates utopian and pastoral modes. If the neighborhood represents "a map
of the future bastard metropolis" (86; 109), it is a city model with
curiously archaic features. The landscape is resolutely urban
(consider the chapter entitled "Don't Talk to Me About the Country"). The cultural mix and the wide range of opportunities exist
only in the metropolis. But the intermingling of public and pri-
vate (86; 109), the emphasis on fertility (85 and 134; 108 and
165), the protagonist's sense of being nurtured by his surround-
ings (134; 165) are properties of the pastoral. It is an odd pastoral,
marked by poverty and rapacity. But there is a lack of hypocrisy
about it (86; 109), this life stripped down to essentials, that
makes it roughly equivalent—at least Goytisolo portrays it as
such—to the simpler, more authentic life the pastoral extols.

Most importantly, Goytisolo's representation of the Sentier
shares with the pastoral, but not with the utopia, a sense of
spontaneity that is the payoff for the absolutely minimal organi-
zation. Goytisolo depicts the Sentier as "a proliferating, madre-
poric chaos" (29; 42), which "instead of being marked off in neat
squares, spontaneously adapts itself to the caprices of chance
and improvisation" (133; 164–65). Since it repels the few officers
who venture there, it is largely unpoliced (133; 165), and it has
been ignored by planners:

no monarch, president, official architect, or urban planner has proposed for it any model of conviviality or recreation whatsoever. To tell the truth, the quarter has not been planned by anyone: it has wisely improvised itself. (41; 56)[6]

Operating on the margins of Western society and virtually uncontrolled, the Sentier enjoys a measure of freedom unknown to the "better" neighborhoods: the freedom to invent itself.

In this schema, "the perfectly ordered Cartesian perspectives of Baron Haussmann" (120; 149)—what is usually regarded as the quintessential Paris—are a utopian project gone (necessarily) awry. Haussmann's boulevards provide a negative urban model to which the Sentier will be explicitly and repeatedly opposed. Ideated by the bourgeois monarchy, the boulevards were cut through the densely populated nucleus of medieval Paris not only in an attempt to bring the light of modernity to the city but also to disperse potentially subversive elements and to facilitate military action in case there were uprisings. Goytisolo insists on the point, referring to "the Paris of the Bourbons and the Bonapartes, planned by its architects in such a way as to dampen potential social explosions" (85; 108). As part of his effort to modernize old Paris and to make it "a fully spectacularised and efficiently policed center of Imperial civilization" (Prendergast 1991, 183), Haussmann promoted the installation of lighting in public places. Early projects for public illumination were inspired by the eighteenth-century belief in universal enlightenment (Buck-Morss 1989, 308). This process is associated with systematized education, which is itself, Northrop Frye points out, regarded as the basis of most utopias (1965, 335–336). Policing, lighting, and controlled enlightenment are related to each other and to the city's archival function. Butor argues that the importance of this last function is such that "the center of authority is not the seat of the government, the military commander, the high priest, it is the archives" (my translation, 1985, 73).

For Goytisolo, this accumulation of texts—high end of the cultural code that constitutes Western society—involves authority in both senses of the term. Hence comes the emphasis on armed force, a connection that recalls Georges Bataille's argument that the museum was invented to replace the beheaded king (Hollier 1989, xiii). The protagonist of *Paisajes*, we are told,

not only disdains the artistic, monumental ensemble—rigorously
laid out so as to forestall the slightest inclination toward efferves-
cence or disorder—extending from the Palais Royal to the Place de
la Concorde, but his aforementioned attitude of rejection also applies
to libraries, theaters, exhibitions, museums. The massive silhouette
of the Louvre—inhospitable and threatening as that of a fortress of
Knowledge—nauseates him. (52; 69)

The only museum the protagonist can tolerate is the Grevin, a
reductio ad absurdum of the discourse that justifies the Louvre
and the National Library. This Parisian House of Wax both com-
pletes and contests the premises that lie behind the official archives. It contains a disorganized and almost hallucinatory
conglomeration of oddities. In addition to a Hall of Mirrors, a
Brahmin Temple, an Enchanted Boat, and an Audience at the
Vatican, it boasts "a potpourri of Charlemagne, Saint Louis, Napoleon, Joan of Arc, Marie Antoinette, the Dauphin, Julio Iglesias,
Richelieu, and Mrs. Thatcher" (53; 70). It revels in the historical
and at the same time subverts any rational, linear articulation of
history by undermining the authority normally associated with
such representations.

This reduction of the past to a grab bag or collage is a gesture
characteristic of postmodernism (Jameson 1991, 361 and 368) as
well as a form of popular entertainment. It is paralleled by the
protagonist's anti-archive, which involves both pieces he has
clipped or copied from the newspapers and the record of his
excursions, real or imaginary, into the city. These "takes" on, or
investigations into, modern life provide an alternative version
of history that focuses (albeit not exclusively) on the dystopias
produced by wrong-headed ideologies, beginning and ending
with monumental Paris, that incontrovertible fact against which
the narrative repeatedly butts its head. Like the Musée Grevin,
this archive is "a landscape of ideological ruins" (124; 153).

Goytisolo's distrust of regimentation is an inheritance of the
Franco years, but also a quality common to postmodernism, as
Jameson points out (1991, 335). It leads him to portray every
planned society as a dystopia: not only the modernized and efficiently policed Paris, but also Albania, where all minds think
alike; Disneyland, a prepubescent paradise; and, of course, Stalin's Russia, which keeps the public enthralled by providing the

excitement of a horror movie in an update of the bread-and-circuses routine. Goytisolo's depictions of Albania and Disneyland share a kind of goofy charm. But Disneyland makes patent the assumption he sees as essential to any such utopian project no matter what the ideological framework: that the population has no mind of its own. This is easiest in the case of Disney, where the utopians are stuffed.[7]

In line with Goytisolo's rejection of the ordered society is his dissatisfaction with political programs, right and left. In numerous essays he has accused them of authoritarianism and lack of imagination.[8] He caricatures them here as absurd (namely, the series of terrorist groups, whose claims cancel each other out) and repressive (Stalin, Lenin, Pol Pot, Trujillo, Franco, Hoxha) or just fatuous (the French intellectuals).[9] The novel's connection to Andrzej Wajda's mocking indictment of postwar politics in the film *Krajobraz po bitwie* (*Landscape after Battle*, 1970) is quite clear. The film takes place in a displaced-persons camp in Germany in 1945. Wajda treats the patriots with sarcasm, their notion of loyalty to the "old" Poland as ridiculous. Faced with the dilemma of returning to a homeland now under Communist authority or going into exile in the West, the protagonist is adrift; there is no good choice in a world that seems bereft of meaningful commitment. In the novel, Paris itself becomes a displaced-persons camp, in which the protagonist is the principal exile. The fidelity of his ex-comrades to a Spain that has long since disappeared seems childish—they are accused of "infantile leftist deviation" (62; 81). But post-Franco Spain, submerged in the confusion following the Tejero revolt in 1981 and dedicated to conspicuous consumption, does not inspire much confidence either in this 1982 novel.

Equally unacceptable are the radical chic politics of the intellectual left in France, pictured here as just so much twaddle. When the cultural establishment turns out in support of Polish miners, the result is farce. In "A Night at the Opera," only those who have the proper "ideological pedigree" and who possess "the indispensable requisite of a literary and artistic sensibility" (121; 150) are invited to the Opéra to attend the protest gala, where face-to-face flattery—"I've devoured your latest novel"—alternates with behind-the-back stabbings—"a failure, a real shit" (121–22; 151). Along with statesmen, artists, intellectuals, and television personalities, the gathering includes figures out of literature: "the Duke and Duchess of Guermantes, Sénécal, Madame Verdurin, Reynaldo Hahn; characters out of Cortázar and Carpentier" (122; 151). In this reified culture, producer and product are equally "unreal."

In fact, in the postcataclysmal world of the novel—the battle in question remains suggestively ambiguous, "a possible natural hecatomb, an unfortunate atomic explosion" (102; 127)—every traditional form of commitment, whether political, artistic or personal—the religious does not even enter into the picture here—is suspect. *Paisajes* takes place on the day of Louis Aragon's funeral (28 December 1982). Goytisolo seizes on Aragon here because of his position as "monument familier" (*Le Monde*, 26–27 December, 6). After his surrealist period, Aragon had become "official bard" (15; 25) of the extremely conservative French Communist party, and the verses exalting the worker, France, and his wife in "Elsa mon amour" are "memorized in all the schools of the land" (15; 25–26).[10]

The street scene suggests just how cut off from the here and now are both the later Aragon's high-flown sentiments and his earlier attempts to domesticate the city space in *Le Paysan de Paris*. The mourners gathered on one side of the boulevard Saint-Denis are reduced to hollow forms: "a double row of black overcoats, hats and fur caps held respectfully in hand" (15–16; 26). On the other side of the street, people are queuing to get into the Horror Film Festival taking place at the porn house. The verses intoned from across the street mean nothing to them:

> neither the black streetsweeper nor the modest, bovine Portuguese couple nor the girl with hennaed hair nor the fake California hippie . . . know who the Red Lady is, nor the passionate poet exalting her. Could they be making a film, maybe, or might it be some sort of elaborate publicity stunt? (16; 26)

Only the black sweeper is touched by the lines, hearing in them a reference to "L'Sa Monammú," famous African seer, a connection that is itself surreal since it shows how the imagination can impose itself on the world.[11]

Both the presence of immigrants in huge numbers and the advent of mass culture contest the notions of stability inherent in an official discourse that espouses traditional values (see Jameson 1991, 16–18). If cultural diversity tends to rob these icons of any recognizable meaning, the culture industry reduces them to articles of consumption (see Debord 1977). There is, then, no common ground for communication in a society over-taken by "the babelization of the great cities" and the cultivated forgetfulness of consumer culture.

The terms are very clear in the fantasy sequence involving the convergence of "maxi-editors y superagents" (88; 111) at the tomb of the Unknown Soldier. The unveiling of that hero is to unleash a huge publicity campaign that will capitalize on his life story (literary, television, film, and product rights), promoting the heroic virtues of the French citizenry in an orgy of commercial-ism. When that traditional hero is revealed to be "a robust black" (92; 116), the French establishment is left high and dry, their notion of an essential national identity discredited.[12] For the publicity people, however, it is a win-win situation: they get in touch with Alex Haley (92; 106).

Like the society it attacks, *Paisajes* is bathed in the aura of commercial culture. It is made up of heterogeneous texts that ape the language and form of ad copy, promos, hack journalism, sitcoms, dime-store romances, pornography, thrillers, slapstick comedies, horoscopes, self-help manuals, lonely-hearts col-umns, and literary criticism. These texts purport to be the pro-tagonist's clippings from and letters to the newspaper. Along with sequences involving his sallies (real or imagined) into the city, they form his investigations into modern city life. The short chapters, set off by jaunty headlines, create a space like a news-paper (the file of clippings) or a television variety show (*Monty Python?*), interrupted by commercials. Here the old "universals" concerning art and the human condition are consumed and re-gurgitated as clichés, TV talk, or—at their toniest—therapeutic doses of high culture (69; 52).

The novel becomes, then, a game involving the shuffling and combination of received ideas. This game wreaks havoc on any traditional notion of mimesis because it reduces representation to repetition, and the object itself to a simulacrum. It exposes as fictions the principles by which we organize our perceptions of ourselves and the world. This approach, which is integral to

Paisajes, has extensive repercussions on every facet of the novel, including what interests us here: the presentation of place.

First of all, Goytisolo's Paris has been overtaken by commercialism. The view from the protagonist's garret (what else?) embraces the Opéra, looking like marzipan and bracketed between a forest of television antennas and the towers of la Défense with its corporate headquarters. The streets are littered with wrappers from McDonald's, McCookin's, and What-A-Burger's. The subway tunnels are plastered with ads for shampoo, cheese, spaghetti, and Club Med. The newsstand sells magazines featuring Julio Iglesias. The Louvre is flooded with Japanese tourists who gaze at the Mona Lisa through mirrored sunglasses. As we have seen in "Maxi-editors and Superagents" and "A Night at the Opera," the cultural establishment has sold out to commercial interests. What could be part of a realistic portrayal of the city is here pushed almost to the point of hallucination. The culture represented in advertising is, in any event, unreal. So this insistence on the commercial tends to make the city seem illusory and insubstantial.

Then, too, Goytisolo's descriptions point less at the city than at themselves. They take forms affected both by film and television techniques and by the kitsch tone that pervades advertising. Some scenes have the cursory, shorthand sound of set descriptions in movie treatments:

> The building has long been a brothel for immigrants, with a dark, rickety spiral staircase. The Moslem hermit-saint's visitors wait patiently on the landing, outside the door of his little cubbyhole: women swathed in shawls and caftans, hands and hair dyed with henna, silent individuals lost in thought. (39; 53)

The landscapes are resolutely urban: the protagonist argues that the Balard metro line is "the most pleasant, the most varied, the most romantic landscape in all of the north of France" (77; 97). These landscapes have a gritty, film noir feel to them without the nostalgia (although the chase scene in "Urban Palimpsest" is straight B-movie). Some descriptions have a nutty kind of camp quality, as does the long discussion of the social strata that comprise the Sentier. This socioeconomic dissection of the neighborhood recalls Balzac's detailed examination of the class/floor distinctions in Madame Vauquer's boarding house, except that here the social strata are compared to the layers of a cake. The confectionery image carries over to "the circular cake of the Opéra and its apparently edible cupola" (8; 17). In both cases, the object is undermined. The piece of cake seems anything but solid. These schlock descriptions that tend to trivialize the object while emphasizing the process of representation remind us that we are, then, dealing with fictional constructs.[13]

The entire monumental complex, we are told here, is made of papier mâché (85; 108); that is, a simulacrum formed of paper, a text. The novel is full of playful allusions to earlier works—the classics that are shredded and reformed to make this "book-city" (my translation, Goytisolo 1988, 36). The protagonist's inventory of clichés includes bits and pieces of a wide range of the literatures that constitute our Western heritage. That tradition serves much the purpose here that the Scripture did for medieval parodists, according to Bakhtin: "This [sacred] word, its style and the way it means, became an object of representation, both word and style were transformed into a bounded and ridiculous image" (75). In this popularizing context, the allusions take on the air of Classic Comics, and their introduction in unexpected but all too likely circumstances is invariably humorous. In Goytisolo's hands, classic literature becomes a joke.

There are so many allusions, and they are so apparently casual, that they give the work the zany quality of a series of improvised skits pulled together from whatever material comes to hand. "In the Shadow of Vladimir Ilich," for example, involves the protagonist's encounter with the political friends from his youth. The setting is Proustian: an autumnal landscape, an ancient mansion. The title in Spanish, "A la sombra de Vladimir Ilich," echoes "A l'Ombre des jeunes filles en fleurs." The protagonist rejects his former friends because of their puerility (they are literally big babies, dressed in playsuits and sailor hats). He tries instead to find solace in the arms of one of the playful little girls about whom he dreams. But he cannot seem to escape from his ex-comrades, who are now encased in garbage cans (a Beckettian touch) and condemned to continue "rotting forever, each in his own garbage can, in the pestilential dung heap of History" (63; 81): they are stuck in *le temps perdu*.[14]

Direct references to "the novelistic heroes of Carpentier or Cor-

tázar" (85; 107) also have an improvised character, as do throw-
away lines like the casual reference to "holy families" with their
children (14; 24). Whenever these obvious readymades are used
(and this applies not only to literary texts but to the received
ideas and images of mass culture—that is, to everything that
comes, as Bakhtin puts it, "with conditions attached" (1981,
75)—the effect is to call attention to the process of representation. The same effect comes from the numerous intradiegetic
references to "the individual this narrative concerns" (28; 41),
"our character" (52; 68), "our protagonist" (58; 76), "the protagonist of this story" (82; 63), "our atrabilious character" (70; 90),
"our excentric character" (86; 109), or "our hero" (24, 28, 45, 63,
89, and 132; 36, 40, 61, 82, 112, and 163).

Some of the texts on which Goytisolo draws provide not just
a sound bite or a knowing nudge to the reader but an underlying
pattern for the novel. This strategy is clearly the case with *Bouvard et Pécuchet*, which is treated with uncharacteristic respect.
It supplies not only the idea of an investigation into modern life
and the catalog of received ideas, as we have seen, but also the
notion, fondly entertained by Bouvard, that Europe can be saved
through Africa.

Goytisolo acknowledges the informing presence of Flaubert's
novel in the epigraph. He is not always so straightforward. Although he refers repeatedly to Lewis Carroll, he is referring to
the Reverend Dodgson's penchant for photographing young girls
in the buff. (The protagonist, who has gotten hold of a volume
of these photographs, likes to imagine himself in Dodgson's
shoes.) The author never refers to *Alice in Wonderland*. Yet Goytisolo's version of the labyrinth (an image endemic to city fiction)
owes its particular contours to Carroll's Wonderland. That Wonderland lies underground, like the Paris metro (the setting for
many sequences in the novel). Alice suffers bewildering transformations there (as does Goytisolo's protean protagonist). And a
peculiar logic obtains in those domains, a logic that often resides
in the animation of dead metaphors and received ideas (the mock
turtle, for instance). Considered literally, these heretofore inert
linguistic forms take on a slightly menacing life of their own,
not unlike the re-energized clichés in *Paisajes*. The tone of both
books is poised somewhere between the nightmarish and the
fun.

Borges, too, contributes to this labyrinth. "In the Paris of Fork-ing Paths," the title of the section dealing with the protagonist's perusal of the metro map, is flip, but the intent is serious. In "The Garden of Forking Paths," Borges envisages a novel that is itself a labyrinth and "an incomplete, but not false, image of the world" composed of

> infinite series of times, in a growing, vertiginous network of diver-gent, convergent and parallel times. That web of times that draw together, fork away, cross each other or for centuries are unaware of each other, covers *every* possibility. (My translation, 1954, 2:109–110)

Borges's network provides an incomplete but not false image of *Paisajes* and explains the fragmented subject's shifts in iden-tity (from sedentary archivist, to would-be seducer of little Alices, to Oteka terrorist) and the equally fragmented plot. This reference helps establish a critical connection between the laby-rinth (or city), the book, and the life of the protagonist. In this chapter, Borges's notion of a space (the labyrinth, the physical book) that is traveled or read or written in time is shorn of its rather exotic trimmings and popularized in the form of a metro map "distributed free to users of the Paris public transport sys-tem" (87; 109). That map is an article of mass consumption that opens the imagination to innumerable trajectories and serves as a mini–version of the novel itself.

Cortázar, as well, is important to the novel. We have already seen how Goytisolo uses references to him—along with Balzac, Proust, and Carpentier—as a way of evoking an image of legend-ary Paris and at the same time suggesting the banality of that image. He is especially hard on Carpentier and Cortázar. Parody tends to simplify, but in the case of Cortázar the author may also have a hidden agenda. It does not take much imagination to see *Paisajes* as a late-twentieth-century update of *Rayuela*. There are, of course, important differences: the presence of the mass media and the third world masses in *Paisajes*; the love element in *Ray-uela* (reduced in *Paisajes* to pornography and a distant, perhaps altogether imaginary, wife). But they both take Paris as the point of departure for an attack on the literary and cultural traditions of the West, and both use parody against those traditions as a way of undermining them and of making the language fresh again. Too, Goytisolo insists that the Sentier is heretofore unmediated—"with no literary past whatsoever" (85; 107). However, his representation of that neighborhood is based on the notion purveyed by Cortázar and the surrealists that the city is a mysterious text which can only be read by the adept. Compare, for example, Goytisolo's contention, cited earier, that the walls of the buildings in the Sentier and the corridors of the metro "offer all sorts of invitations and solicitations to anyone who wishes or knows how to read them" (29; 42), with Cortázar's comment that Oliveira "guesses that in some part of Paris, some day or some death or some meeting will show him a key" (133; 160). And compare it too with Aragon's comment in *Le Paysan de Paris* that "I had lively hopes that a lock to the universe was at my fingertips, if only the bolt were suddenly to slip" (94).

In fact, *Paisajes*, like *Rayuela*, owes more than it would admit to surrealism (this fact may help explain the dig at Aragon). Both novels are closely related to the Walk (Brown, Afterward to Aragon 1970, 169), a genre typified by *Nadja* and *Le Paysan de Paris*, both of which are structured around a saunter through the city that allows the mind to wander,[15] pausing at will to study what it encounters. The objects and scenes that lie in the path of the *flaneur*-hero may serve as springboards for meditation. Or they may be incorporated into the body of the text as realia or transformed by means of the hallucinatory image—the cornerstone of the surrealists' effort to renew the word—into something quite different. *Le Paysan* includes signboards, menus, price lists, playbills, and public notices. It also includes a mixture of styles and genres: stretches of automatic writing, scraps of poetry, little plays, gossip, philosophical discourse, and hallucinatory sequences, the most notable involving the transformation of a shopwindow filled with walking sticks (a most appropriate choice) into an undersea fantasy.

Paisajes shares an obvious resemblance to these compendia of the literary, the subliterary, and the extraliterary. It, too, maintains tension between "the twin poles of libidinous fantasy and random observation" (Collier 1985, 223), so that common scenes are subjected to hallucinatory changes, and the most banal of circumstances may be invested with meaning by *le hasard objectif* (L'Sa Monnamu). But what is different in *Paisajes* is the tone and the intent. Aragon and Breton are enthusiastic proselytes of the modern, who tend to the portentious in their conviction that "the face of the infinite" lies beneath the concrete forms of the city (Aragon 1970, 95); Aragon connects the modern explicitly with the unconscious (102). For Goytisolo, the modern is what goes without saying. He is far more skeptical about the power of the unconscious, which here seems more like a receiver of packaged "presentations," including the discourse of surrealism.

All of these allusions in *Paisajes*, whether literary or extraliterary, direct or hidden, make for a multilayered, poly-semantic text dependent on the interanimation of a wide variety of discourses that mimics the social and physical interaction essential to metropolitan life. Although the novel makes a point of the breakdown in consensus, it demands an urbane reader conversant with a wide variety of idiolects. Unless these quotations retain a trace of difference, the relentless leveling process to which Goytisolo subjects art, culture, and politics will be meaningless. He uses the techniques of mass culture—the flip or coy or platitudinous tone, the flattening of complexity, the quick take or channel switching, the abrupt changes in tone and format—to democratize the text and undermine the foundations of official culture. He obviously feeds off the energy and gets a kick out of manipulating the clichés of mass culture. But he also turns it inside out to expose the uniformity and shallowness commercial culture imposes on life in the late twentieth century, as well as to condemn the profit motive that drives it.

One of his charges against politicians is their failure to question either "the idea that industrialization liberates human beings" or "the more and more suicidal aberrations of the consumer society" (my translation, Goytisolo 1978, 78). The poverty of recent immigrants to the Sentier—Afghans, Pakistanis, and Bangladeshis, herded like cattle from one miserable job to another—serves as an eloquent rebuke to the conspicuous consumption represented by ads promoting status symbols. So, too, do the nuclear holocaust scenarios that function much as biblical prophecies. The leveling tendency, which Goytisolo uses so effectively to subvert exalted notions of high culture, is part of that process of North-Americanization that would destroy all cultural diversity, converting the Unknown Soldier, for example, into another Abe Lincoln (89; 113) and the impoverished residents of the Sentier into frustrated consumers.[16]

In reaction to the powerful influence that this consumer society exercises over everyone, including those who cannot function effectively unless they are disinterested, Goytisolo posits a different kind of thinker: "the wandering Sufi dervish" (149; 183). This figure cultivates despicable habits in order to cut himself off entirely from the blandishments that would seduce him as they do the co-opted artists and intellectuals convened for "A Night at the Opera" and excoriated throughout the novel.[17] The protagonist, who fits this description to a T, is intended, then, as an exemplum, necessarily grotesque, of intellectual and artistic integrity in a reified culture. The story of his trajectory from the trammels of bourgeois respectability to the freedom of the pariah is a new kind of spiritual autobiography that stands the genre on its head by inverting its standard itinerary. Here sanctity (in its usual sense) is equated with sanctimoniousness, and sin is essential to salvation. The whiny, platitudinous voice of the "we" narrator represents what the protagonist is still in the process of leaving behind. It is the policeman that Goytisolo says he once carried inside and that demands "an internal, not external, battle against . . . the intimate censorship that is part of 'the mechanism of the soul'" (1978, 16). The numerous parodic references to Proust suggest that for the protagonist of *Paisajes*, unlike Proust's narrator, *le temps perdu* is best forgotten.

As the protagonist's name and teasing bits of data indicate this "deliberately grotesque autobiography" (149, 184) is a version of the author's life as well. In an interview with Randolph Pope, Goytisolo describes the protagonist as "a gentleman who lives in my neighborhood, lives in my house, lives in my room, who could be me, but isn't" (my translation, 1985, 125). Yet the similarities are more notable than the differences. Like his burlesque double, the author sees his life as an effort to escape the prejudices that came with growing up in a relatively affluent Barcelona family. He writes, for example, using the third person, about the effort of "freeing himself successively from his political, patriotic, social and sexual tabus" (my translation, 1975, 16). His separation from Spain, his peripatetic existence (he divides his time between the Sentier, New York, and Marrakech and travels extensively to other places), his adoption of the Arab cause—all these factors serve to align the author with his intellectual ideal, the dervish, and with the protagonist, who is the comic representation of that ideal.[18]

In the novel, the development in time of the protagonist is paralleled by a translation in space "from the hamlet to the medina" (136; 168); from Barcelona, "a bourgeois, monochrome, homogeneous milieu," where the protagonist is raised, to the Sentier, "popular, hybrid, and motley" (137; 169), where he reaches maturity. His intellectual ideal, represented by the dervish, is related to Arab culture, which predominates in this representation of the Sentier (although Goytisolo insists on the mixture of non-Western cultures that are housed therein). According to Nadjm Oud-Dine Bammamu, nomad cultures like the Arabic are, by definition, cultures of transcendence. They hold that "it is not proper to amass objects, much less have a sentimental attachment to them. Those around one must be on loan, temporarily held on someone else's behalf, and as precarious as life itself;" the Christian culture, in contrast, "has its roots in the peasantry, which possesses things it passes on in the form of an inheritance" (1977, 48). In the novel, Christians are engaged in an orgy of conspicuous consumption, an individual manifestation of the national urge to accumulate territory that is represented in the ex-colonials who now populate the Sentier. The Arab (at least in theory) is free of that itch.

Thus, the geographic opposition between Haussmann's Paris and the Sentier parallels the psychic opposition between property and respectability, on the one hand, and, on the other, freedom. The layout of the city is also the layout of a life. Since Goytisolo treats Haussmann's Paris as an extension of Barcelona—they share the same wide boulevards and the same bourgeois ethos—it represents the constraints that informed his earlier life, whereas the Sentier stands for the marginal, exilic existence he has chosen to lead. Goytisolo insists on the point: "the microcosm of Le Sentier, the microcosm of his own life" (63; 82), "a map of the future bastard metropolis that at the same time will be the map of his own life" (86; 109), "to examine the map of the métro is . . . to visit the monuments, the abominations, the horrors of the city, one's own monuments, abominations, and horrors" (87; 110). This almost mystical correspondence between the city and the life of the protagonist includes a third term—the book itself, which is both biography and map: "you may stroll through the streets write lose your way in the double space of the city and the book" (157; 192). The book, which is a collage, imitates both the experience of the city and the fragmented nature of the protagonist, who is simultaneously an Oteka terrorist, a pornographer, a writer on scientific subjects, and an archivist.[19] Finally, in a sequence that parodies *Cien años de soledad*, city, protagonist, and book are destroyed, only—and this, of course, is the nature of fiction—to begin again.

Perhaps ultimately the real utopia in *Paisajes* is not the physical Sentier, but what it represents in terms of psychic and creative freedom. It might be more accurate to say that the *locus amoenus* is the text itself. It is a space that allows for the suspension of normal logic and the happy combination of deliriously heterogeneous elements. It is a space that, momentarily at least, supplants the stubborn reality of a Paris where the street signs are not written in Arabic and the Sentier is just a peripheral neighborhood. It is a space that founds its own city, "a book-city," governed only by the dictates of desire.

Conclusion
A Portion of Paris

IN "EL RASTRO DE TU SANGRE EN LA NIEVE," (YOUR BLOOD TRAIL IN THE snow) which forms part of *Doce cuentos peregrinos* (1992), García Márquez describes a young Colombian set adrift in Paris after his new bride is beset by a mysterious illness. Wandering the city in a state of some confusion, Billy Sánchez spots the Eiffel Tower, "and it seemed so close that he tried to reach it walking along the quais. But soon he realized that it was farther away than it seemed and, worse yet, it kept changing places" (my translation, 222). The mysterious movements of the tower, that emblem of Paris, suggest the simultaneously tantalizing and elusive nature of the city itself in the narratives examined here.

All these narratives play off an idealized notion of the city, whether that ideal is located on the grand boulevards or on the Left Bank and whether it is affirmed or, much more commonly, denied. *Rayuela* takes place in the fifties' Bohemia of the Left Bank, a psychic space frozen into a self-conscious simulacrum of itself. *La juventud en la otra ribera* suggests that this Left Bank Bohemia is not just self-conscious, but a deliberate falsification, a stage set designed to entice mass tourism and to dupe the unwary. *El recurso del método* and *Una familia lejana* bypass the Bohemian image to evoke the apparent stasis of monumental Paris. In both novels, the city is metonymized in a closed space: the Dictator's mansion, on the one hand, and the Automobile Club of France, on the other. In *Reencuentro de personajes*, the city goes almost undescribed; it is beautiful but cold, a kind of reverse Bohemia where freedom from the constraints of home offers the chance not to realize a potential for the best but for the worst. Finally, *Paisajes después de la batalla* depends on a series of oppositions between the boulevards and Bohemia, reconstituted here in the Sentier, and it happily envisages a time

111

when the "most capital of capitals," to use Darío's phrase, goes up in flames.

That these narratives gravitate toward one or both of the two most widely disseminated images of the city—Bohemian Paris and Beau Monde Paris—suggests not only that the authors are interested in exploring the idealized city's promise of fulfillment, and I shall return to this point. But they also want to call attention to the commodification of the Parisian experience. Treating the city as a tourist spectacle perceived (and ultimately fictionalized) by outsiders is a way to draw attention to the conventional nature of representation in general and to remind us of the artificial nature of cultural practices. The choice of viewing this system of meanings as constructed rather than inherent allows the writers to subvert the hegemonic discourse of the center—Paris, Europe—by insisting on the interpretive competence of the periphery. Thus, in *Una familia* the Caribbean Heredia's understanding of French history is as justifiable as Branly's, despite the latter's impeccable French credentials. And Verónica's reading of Waugh and Fitzgerald in *Reencuentro* is as valid as more traditional English or North American interpretations. Finally, it means the enfranchisement of all these far-flung authors as interpreters of the Paris scene.

The city that emerges in their representations, for all the differences in angle of vision, is bounded by certain constants. It is, as we have seen, presented quite consciously as textual, not actual, a palimpsest composed of innumerable descriptions, in literature, history, and art. It is also a Paris populated by foreigners. From Oliveira's fellow Beats in *Rayuela* (a Russian, a Chinese, two North Americans, a Uruguayan, one Frenchman, and their literary hero, an Italian) to the third world immigrants and first world tourists in *Paisajes*, the Paris depicted in these novels is notable for the minimal role played by—at times the virtual absence of—the French. Most of the characters, like the authors and like the texts themselves, fall somewhere in between—between nationalities, between languages, between literatures. In this sense, the form of the novel follows the layout of the city, which is cosmopolitan, multivocal, fragmented, and dispersed. Of these works, only *La juventud* appears to function as a traditional narrative (the quest), and it does so only to subvert that form.

It is not really surprising that such carefully constructed frag-

mentation should coexist with a paradoxical longing for wholeness. If the one reflects the city and the world that confront us
today, the other reflects the no less real desire to surmount the
limitations of that world. And it is perhaps inevitable in novels
that take place in Paris that this longing should be related to the
city's utopian potential. It may be a false or failed utopia—like
the Bohemia purveyed to Dr. Huamán or the static perfection of
Belle Epoque Paris that eventually rejects Carpentier's Dictator
or the dystopia where Garro's Véronica finds only the freedom
to be abused. Or it may refer to the surrealists' belief in Paris as
a field of providential conjunctions, those unions of opposites
that are the source of meaningful experience. For Oliveira in
Rayuela, the ideal is artistic and psychological, the realization
of a new way of writing and a new way of being. But he uses a
utopian metaphor—"the city"—to describe this psychic space,
and he relates it to the kind of serendipitous encounters that
Paris facilitates. For Fuentes, the ideal is social as well as psychic—a harmony based on acknowledging, rather than repress-
ing, the other. He sees it represented in Supervielle's happy
fusion of French and Latin American currents in his poetry and
also by the presence of Latin American writers working in Paris.
Goytisolo relates the ideal both to the mysterious life of the Sentier, a microcosm of "the future bastard metropolis" (in other
words, a synthesis of others, 1987, 86; 1982, 109), and to the
psychic freedom that living in the Sentier means for the writer
himself.

These visions of inclusion—the union of opposites, the acceptance of the other—may ultimately originate in the writers' paradoxical wish for incorporation into just that area they have been
busy deconstructing: the center, the mainstream—what Paris
stands for—and Paris itself. A 1964 essay on urban planning
insists that "it is traditionally an honor for France to have known
how to create a city so open that one can consider oneself a
Parisian, and be recognized as such, without the necessity of
being French" (Alain Griotteray quoted in Evenson 1979, 1). But
against that remark should be weighed comments like Rubén
Darío's "I could never feel anything but an outsider among these
people" (my translation, 1950, 1:464). These representations of
Paris, I believe, are in part a response to the sense of insignifi-
cance and disenfranchisement that is a portion of the foreigner's

lot. They involve an attempt to master, even control, the city. Finally, the utopian space—what I have suggested of *Paisajes* is true for all these projects—the space where the city meets the imaginative demands of the author, in fact *needs* the author and bows to that authority, is the book itself.

The "real" city is so diverse a phenomenon that it seems unreal, a figment that always lies a little beyond our ken and beyond anyone's power of representation. Like Borges's other tiger, it avoids capture. But the word-city—even in these self-conscious narrations—has a reality and a life of its own. These works that show the limits of representation also demonstrate their authors' creative vitality. The fictional world encroaches on the other; the Paris of today registers not only the presence of Rudolph and Mimi, of the Guermantes, of Nadja, but also of Oliveira and la Maga, of the Ex, and of Branly and "Fuentes" and the others. These characters and the fictions that animate them are now an inextricable part of the imaginative warp and woof of Paris. The Eiffel Tower, which eludes poor Billy Sánchez, is caught in the pages of García Márquez's grim fairy tale, just as the Hispanic novels we have studied here catch and hold, if not Paris itself, then a portion of its life in the reader's imagination.

Notes

CHAPTER 1. ANTECEDENTS AND PATTERNS

1. All translations for Carrillo's autobiography are my own.

2. Between 1880 and 1895 its colonial possessions increased from 1.0 to 9.5 million square kilometers and from five to fifty million native inhabitants (Said 1993, 169).

3. The earliest known literary embodiment of the type is Lucio V. López's sketch "Don Polidoro (Retrato de muchos)," dating from 1880. Don Polidoro suffers martyrdom in Paris because of his ignorance of things cultural and his innocence of French, but once back in Buenos Aires he outdoes everyone in tales of his exploits abroad (1915, 349–61). This sketch and a number of the novels that follow it register alarm at the rise of a middle class with money to get to Paris.

4. See Sylvia Molloy (1972), Angel Rama (1977) and Pedro Salinas (1968) for discussions of what Salinas calls "the Paris complex" (32). José Luis Romero refers to the importance of Paris in relation to the ostentatious or rastacuero style of life adopted by the newly affluent middle classes in the last decades of the nineteenth century and first decades of the twentieth (1976).

5. For the attraction Paris exerted on foreigners during Sarmiento's time, see Lloyd S. Kramer's Threshold of a New World: Intellectuals and the Exile Experience in Paris, 1830–1848 (1988).

6. About a third of José Bianco's La pérdida del reino takes place in Paris, but this novel, written in the fifties, was not published until 1972. Eduardo Mallea's La bahía de silencio (1940) follows the protagonist to Europe, including a brief stay in Paris. In both cases, representation is treated as transparent, providing the reader with a faithful copy of reality.

7. I am misusing a line from Gertrude Stein, who said this, with a different intention, of Oakland, California, in Everybody's Autobiography (1973, 289).

8. That such an approach can prove fruitful has been amply demonstrated in Imagining Paris: Exile, Writing, and American Identity (1993), J. Gerald Kennedy's study of the ways in which their experience of Paris affected the careers of the North American writers resident there during the early modernist period.

9. In Street Noises: Parisian Pleasure, 1900–40 (1993), Adrien Rifkin discusses the depiction of Paris as a woman and the idealization of the popular as a form of social alterity. See especially chapters 2 and 4 of this work. In Shari Benstock's Women of the Left Bank, there is also a brief discussion of the depiction of Paris as a woman ("The Patriarchal Perspective: Paris Is a Woman," 1986, 447–48).

10. Sarmiento announces that "I am equal to Paris. . . . I have been initiated

into its secrets. I know what only a few know" (my translation, quoted in Viñas, 1964, 40).

11. See my chapter on *Rayuela* for an extended discussion of this image.

CHAPTER 2. THE CITY AS TEXT: READING PARIS IN *RAYUELA*

1. I have used Gregory Rabassa's translation for all quotations from this novel. The page number of the translation is given first, followed by the page number of the Spanish edition that is cited in the bibliography.

2. As Bakhtin has pointed out, the sort of novel that questions its own discourse often focuses this critique on the hero, a reader who tries to mold his life according to literature; Don Quixote and Emma Bovary are the first examples that come to mind (1981, 413).

3. I am indebted to Hutcheon for much of my discussion of parody. See especially her chapter 2. Cortázar must also have been interested in Breton's attempt to write a new kind of book and to mold a new kind of reader.

4. The idea that each arrondissement offers a different take on the sexual experience is exploited in Pierre MacOrlan's *Images secrètes de Paris* (1922), a descriptive catalog of the brothel or type of prostitution typical of each of the twenty arrondissements.

5. Morelli exasperated them because he offered something close to hope, to justification, "but at the same time denied them total security, keeping them in an unbearable ambiguity" (535; 604).

6. The point here is well summed up by Irving Howe, who comments that "in *Ulysses* and *The Trial* the traditional journeys of the hero are replaced by a compulsive backtracking; there is no place else to go, and the protagonist's motions within the city stand for his need, also through backtracking, to find a center within self" (1971, 64).

7. This notion of the key brings to mind a passage from Pierre Véry's *Les Métamorphoses*, in which Fantômas's possession of "all the keys" shows his mastery of the city. "Notre Dame, night. An axial altar. The man with dark glasses [Fantómas] is here. He has the keys to the sacristy, and the verger, an accomplice, lights his way with a candle. The Louvre. The portrait of Mona Lisa flinches. The man with dark glasses appears. He has the keys to the door and to the gate. The guard, who is devoted to him, lights his way with a dark lantern. Now the cellars of the Headquarters of the Police. It is always the same man. The police, who are his creatures, pretend to sleep as he passes by. Once again, he has the keys. He has all the keys" (my translation, 1931, 178–179). It also echoes Sarmiento's remark that he had the key to two doors in Paris: his official recommendation from the Chilean government and his newly published *Facundo* (1981, 118). The second key initially does him little good.

8. See Franco's article (1976) for a discussion of the differences between Paris and "the city."

9. These red rags recall the red scarves that were a part of both the repertoire and the raiment of the Parisian street singers in the first half of this century (see Rifkin, 1993, 185). La Maga has moved to Paris in order to study singing.

CHAPTER 3. DREAMS OF A GOLDEN AGE: *LA JUVENTUD EN LA OTRA RIBERA*

1. All translations from Ribeyro's novella (1983) are my own.

2. What little criticism has been published is not in agreement. Julio Ortega

sees the novella as a fairly straightforward indictment of a world falsified by greed. "So Paris is no longer an 'enigma,' but a mirage," he writes (my trans., 1985, 140). This indictment is presented through the story of the hapless victim, "who believes that he has 'reached that bank, miraculously,' the side of youth, but who has only been tricked" (139). As Ortega sees it, Huamán never realizes what is happening to him. Graciela Coulson, on the other hand, insists that Huamán seeks out his death. "It is obvious that this attitude, this advance toward death, is conscious," she writes (my trans., 1974, 225). Wolfgang Luchting writes of Huamán's "increasing acceptance of—or indifference to—Solange's mysterious plot" (my trans., 1975, 67). For him, "the most important part of La juventud is its exploration of the phenomenon of ambiguity. And this is, in turn, the most important part of Plácido Huamán's European experience; in that region he is an outsider by definition: a foreigner" (1983, 142). Luchting argues that the ambiguity is necessary to what he identifies as the Jamesian theme of the innocent American who falls victim to the corrupt Europeans. Although this is true, it does not explain why the difficulty with which Huamán deciphers his situation in Paris is paralleled by the difficulty with which the reader is forced to decipher this text. Marina Kaplan, with whom I discussed this work at various times, examines it in a particularly interesting essay entitled "The Latin American Romance in Sarmiento, Borges, Ribeyro, Cortázar, and Rulfo," which she was kind enough to let me see in manuscript form just as I was finishing my own essay. We both treat the novella as a romance, although Kaplan relates it specifically to the Latin American romance, which, she argues, attempts "to magically transcend a history portrayed as a grotesque nightmare" (1994, 330). She sees Huamán's adventure as a "ritual combat for social legitimacy" (332) in which, by trying to outwit his opponents, he, like Borges's Lönnrot, unintentionally cooperates in his own murder (332).

3. That as early as the turn of the century such a view had become consumer-directed is confirmed by the number of journalistic reports distributed throughout Latin America and aimed at a broad public.

4. See Guy Debord's argument that in a consumer society the image becomes the ultimate commodity (1977, 35–36).

5. In The Tourist: A New Theory of the Leisure Class (1976), McCannell writes that "touristic consciousness is motivated by its desire for authentic experiences, and the tourist may believe that he is moving in this direction, but often it is very difficult to know for sure if the experience is in fact authentic. It is always possible that what is taken to be entry into a back [i.e., "real"] region is really entry into a front region that has been totally set up in advance for touristic visitation. In tourist settings, especially in industrial society, it may be necessary to discount the importance . . . of front and back regions except as ideal poles of touristic experience" (101).

6. For my discussion of the genre I have relied most heavily on the following works: Northrop Frye, The Anatomy of Criticism (1957) and The Secular Scripture: A Study of the Structure of Romance (1976); Frederic Jameson, "Magical Narratives: Romance as Genre" (1975); and John Stevens, Medieval Romance: Themes and Approaches (1973). For a discussion of the quest in myth, Joseph Campbell, The Hero with a Thousand Faces (1949) is invaluable.

7. The parody romance, which turns, in Northrop Frye's formulation, on "characters confused by romantic assumptions about reality" (1976, 39), is perfectly consonant with the travails of a protagonist like Huamán who seems incapable of adjusting expectation to observation. Frye goes so far as to suggest at this point that all realistic novels may be parody romances. It is clear that he is using the word "parody" in a broad sense.

8. "Ribera" can be either bank or shore. Both meanings come into play in the story.

9. Paul Fussell describes the tourist as "a fantasist equipped temporarily with unaccustomed power" (1980, 42). Removed from the confines of home, Huamán has both the freedom to court Solange and the money to take her out for expensive meals and to buy her presents.

10. The Spanish "juventud" means youth, youthfulness, and young people.

11. The river itself is an ambivalent symbol, drawing together notions of renewal and of death (as in Jorge Manrique's Coplas). For Huamàn, his romantic adventure is a "bath of youthfulness" (305), but it is also "the privileged ark that survived the flood" (282). Borel uses a similar image in expounding his theory of existence: "The most important thing is to enjoy ourselves, as if we were to be shipwrecked, to admire the flowers that grow on the edge of the abyss, and perhaps even to grab one as we fall" (292). The river, then, is both the bath that restores and the flood that destroys.

12. Fontainebleau is known for its outcroppings of sandstone rock. In his diary entry for March 7, 1644, John Evelyn writes that on the way to the palace, "we passed through a forest so prodigiously encompass'd with hideous rocks of whitish hardstone, heaped one on another in mountainous heights, that I think the like is nowhere to be found more horrid and solitary" (quoted in H. A. Piehler 1953, 196).

13. In ancient literature, the psychic danger represented by the loss of rationality was embodied metaphorically in the form of a forest inhabited by wild beasts and women: "While the monster embodies the terror engendered by the hostility of featureless terrain to the rational process, the enchantress . . . incarnates its feminine seductiveness, the temptation for man to yield to anti-rational self-indulgences of the body and spirit, unbridled sexuality or slothful day-dreaming, away from the restraints of his community and its institutions" (Paul Piehler 1971, 73).

14. Frye comments that "in an atmosphere of tragic irony [as opposed to comedy] the emphasis is on spell-binding, linked to a steady advance of paralysis or death" (1976, 131).

15. Salvador Fajardo has suggested to me in conversation that the name may have been inspired by Gontran Paradis, a character in Pierrot, mon ami. Queneau's character lives on the qui vive, but he has little else in common with Ribeyro's sinister figure.

CHAPTER 4. AT HOME ABROAD, ABROAD AT HOME: EL RECURSO
DEL MÉTODO

1. All quotations from the novel are from Frances Partridge's translation (1976). The page numbers of the Spanish edition cited in the bibliography (1974a) are given after the page numbers of the translation.

2. Carpentier refers to it as a "drama de la conciencia." The Spanish conciencia can mean either "conscience" or "consciousness." Since the Illustrious Academic's play concerns "David and Bathsheba, whose nights of love were poisoned by the ghost of Uriah" (26; 29), the more likely reading is "conscience." El recurso, on the other hand, involves an exploration of the dictator's consciousness, but not conscience, of which he has little.

3. Or this one: "There were people these days who collected horrible Afri-

can masks, figures bristling with votive nails, zoomorphic idols—the work of cannibals. . . . Negro musicians were arriving from the United States. That way could only lead us to exalting Attila, Erostratus, the Iconoclasts, the cake-walk, English cooking, anarchist outrages, and the reign of new Circes calling themselves Lyane de Pougy, Emilienne d'Alençon or Cleo de Mérode" (22; 24–25). Here the concatenation of elements from widely different spheres of life demonstrates the Academic's prejudiced reaction to all that involves change— that is, it functions as mimesis—but it also produces a carnival effect. The suggestion that the cakewalk has the same value as the discovery of primitive art or the anarchist movement inevitably calls attention to the *ars combinatoria* shaping the passage.

4. In this regard, see Djelal Kadir's discussion of Carpentier's baroque in *El reino de este mundo*. Kadir sees Carpentier as caught "between the nostalgia for a world of 'faith' with its own logos which, as he desired in his 1949 prologue [to *El reino*], pre-exists rational discourse, and a world of language whose articulation renders the object of its parlance a subversive and self-deflecting schema of textuality" (1986, 103). Along the same lines, González Echevarría observes that "the overall movement of each text is away from litera-ture into immediacy, whether by a claim to be integrated within a larger context, Latin American reality or history, or by an invocation of the empirical author. But because of the dialectics just sketched, the voyage always winds up in literature" (1977, 22). As I shall argue, the move into immediacy is more appar-ent than real; even in the Latin American context, the process of mediation is made manifest.

5. Although the Arc de Triomphe was completed in 1836, the area around the Place de l'Etoile was not built up until the middle of the nineteenth century when it was incorporated into the city. Like most of Haussmann's designs, this section accommodated the increasingly powerful upper middle class; the aristocracy continued to inhabit the old quarters (Saalman 1971, 16 and 44). It is not by chance that Carpentier situates the Prime Minister here. As Romero points out, Haussmann's work inspired the rebuilding of a number of Latin American capitals, and the Second Empire style became a standard among the newly rich for both the mansion and the public building (1976, 274–80).

6. Initially, the painting figures as a piece of nostalgia, but after the massacre in which he becomes known as the "Butcher of Nueva Córdoba" (84; 94), it signifies his social debacle in Paris.

7. All these painters are referred to in the *Dictionnaire critique et docu-mentaire des peintres, sculpteurs, dessinateurs et graveurs* (1953). All, except for Dumont, were members of the Ecole de France. Jean Bérard (1849–1936) "was inspired by modern life to create his own genre" (my translation, 1:567). His paintings can be seen in museums in Liège, Lille, Tours, and Troyes. Paul-Charles Chocarne-Moreau (1855–1931) "likes to introduce some gaiety into his canvases to show the pleasant side of things" (my translation, 2:327), favoring such subjects as chimney sweeps, ragamuffins, and flower girls. He won a bronze medal at the 1889 World's Fair, and the state bought many of his paint-ings. Some of his works hang now in the Musée de Combrai. Although there were a number of Dumonts active at the turn of the century, the one referred to here is probably the genre painter Alfred-Paul-Emile-Etienne Dumont (1828–1894) of the Ecole Suisse. Some of his work is exhibited in the museum at Basel. Jean-León Gérôme (1824–1904), perhaps the best-known painter in the dictator's collection, specialized in historical subjects and is represented in the Louvre and the Wallace Collection, as well as other museums. Henri Gervex

(1852–1929) was famous in his day for his nudes, particularly his *Rolla*. He did the panels in the foyer of the Opéra-Comique and a wall in the Hôtel de Ville, and his *Satyr et Bacchante* hangs in the Louvre. However, "his surest claim to fame is having been one of Renoir's friends" (my translation, 4:223). Finally, Luc-Olivier Merson (1845–1920) painted historical, religious and legendary themes. *Le loup de Gubbio*, probably his best-known painting, is in the museum at Lille. The largest collection of his works hangs in the museum in Chantilly. All of the Prime Minister's paintings contribute to the consolidation of the rich and powerful. Even Chocarne-Moreau's study of a chimney sweep lends itself to the sanctification of the good life by sentimentalizing—i.e., naturalizing—poverty.

8. The scene that involves the Palace of Mirrors in the brothel (mentioned above) has the same effect.

9. See, for example, David Carroll (1987, 116) and Gombrich (1960).

10. In May 1968, as Carpentier surely knew, it was a rallying point for a huge demonstration in support of the regime.

11. Of the devolution of the capital to nature, Carpentier writes: "the new town decreased—that is the word: *decreased* as rapidly as it had increased. What had been large grew smaller, flatter, contracted, as if returning to the clay of its foundations. . . . Unpainted, uncared-for, these buildings combined to make a sort of urban grisaille which degraded, crippled and decomposed the modern part of the town, swathing it in the decay of what had already been old at the beginning of the century. . . . Vast urbanizations and building-lots in the outskirts had been reconquered by the plants descending from the mountains—plants returning to the capital with their bells and festive plumes; and behind them shrubs, and behind the shurbs, trees and tree ferns, all the seedling vegetation of Quick Advance and Quick Growth, shading the small stones among which exiled snakes were now returning to spawn" (219–21; 245–47). Lewis Mumford refers to this process in which the city crumbles and returns to nature by the biological term *Abbau* (1970, 150–52).

12. In an interview that coincided with the publication of the novel, Carpentier commented on his use of Descartes: "there is a constant opposition between [true Cartesianism and a degraded form of Cartesianism] that covers the worst excesses. That is, it is just the opposite of what Descartes had in mind. We've seen too much of that on our continent" (my translation, 1974, 16). Frances Wyers Weber discusses the subject in detail, focusing primarily on the ironic inversion whereby the *Discours de la méthode* serves as a standard for judging the dictator and his methods (1983, 323–34). Wodzimerz Krysinski sees the quotations from Descartes as a meta-narrative that provides a sort of mirror of the semiotic trajectory of the "real narrator" at the same time that the insertion of Descartes's words in the novel leads us to question their value (1987, 394–97). González Echevarría points out that the title also refers to Vico's *ricorsi* and that it is intended to bring to mind not only the *Discours* but the Vico-Descartes debate as well (1977, 258–60).

13. In "El arte narrativo y la magia," Borges argues that "the law of sympathy that postulates an inevitable connection between distant things, either because their form is alike—imitative, homeopathic magic—or because of a prior proximity—contagious magic" holds sway in the novel, which is "a precise game of clues, echoes and affinities [where] every episode . . . has already been prepared for" (my translation, 1954, 1:91). The opera-sugar connection is both imitative and contagious.

14. For studies of Carpentier's appropriation of Proust in the novel, see Dorf-

man (1982) and Faris (1980). Neither of them discusses how the presence of Proustian characters draws attention to the status of *El recurso* as a work of fiction.

15. The plagiarized valediction, incidentally, passes from Caesar to the dictator by way of Rabelais, who appropriated the expression on his own deathbed, but with the significant amendment: "The farce is over," an ending that might have been closer to the mark, if less flattering (*Fleurs* n.d., 9).

16. He tells the story of "the archdeacon, who was enamoured of a gypsy who used to make a white nanny-goat dance to a tambourine . . . and the story of the itinerant poet who egged on some beggars to attack the church . . . and the story of a hunch-backed bell-ringer, who was also in love with the gypsy . . . and the story of two skeletons which seemed to be embracing and were perhaps those of Esmeralda and the bell-ringer . . ." (292; 323–24).

17. Actually, Proust's narrator makes the suggestion at the same time that he denies it: "I dare not say ambitiously 'like a cathedral,' but simply like a dress" (1934, 2:1113).

18. In speaking of farce and comedy, I refer, of course, to Hayden White's discussion of Marx's emplotment of history (1973, 309–17).

19. Oddly enough, *El recurso*'s allegorical potential has made a number of critics uneasy. Ariel Dorfman, for example, writes that in the novel, Carpentier "sketches out a panorama that goes beyond the period, the country or the tyrant himself. But without falling into allegory. . . ." (1982, 107). The problem, I would argue, is not that Carpentier "falls" into allegory, but that he fails to realize the allegory he attempts a bit halfheartedly.

CHAPTER 5. LA CHAMBRE VOISINE: LATIN AMERICA AND PARIS IN *UNA FAMILIA LEJANA*

1. When quoting from the novel, I use Peden's translation (1982). The page number of the Spanish edition (1980) follows the page number of the translation as part of the in-text information.

2. "From start to finish of the novel, the Mexican or Latin American identity has been contrasted with that of France or Europe—with a marked preference given to the latter" (1983, 44). The Latin American presence "constitutes a primitive, bestial, even monstrous other that invades the mind and soul of Fuentes, obliterating the images of refinement and reason that he has attempted to cultivate. . . . The Latin American identity is evoked with excruciating ambivalence" (45). This excerpt is part of a long and interesting article on Fuentes's deployment of the double in *Una familia*. Gyurko does not differentiate here between Fuentes the author and Fuentes the character, and this fact, I believe, leads him to accept the character's Francophilia uncritically.

3. Another tale of terror with a similar aim is *Wide Sargasso Sea* (1966), Jean Rhys's "prequel" to *Jane Eyre*. Rhys contests English cultural traditions by telling the "true history" of Mr. Rochester, romantic hero of the nineteenth-century novel. In Rhys's version, Mr. Rochester marries a beautiful and rich Caribbean girl out of economic necessity, exploits her sexually and economically, and then, when his older brother is killed, returns to England to claim his inheritance. Since the wife is now expendable—he has already gotten his hands on her money, and her sexuality has begun to frighten him—he simply locks her up in the attic like a dirty secret. In her madness and her fate, she

may have been a model for Mademoiselle Lange, who, exploited and then abandoned by her husband, clings to memories of the past, and whose portrait is relegated to the attic at the Clos des Renards.

4. Fuentes reread Proust's work about the time he was beginning the novel. For the influence of Proust in other ways, see Wendy B. Faris's comments (1983, 179–80). She does not refer to the question of memory.

5. Although Fredric Jameson tends to dismiss what he calls "historical fantasy" or "fantastic historiography" as nonserious, he does admit that "new multiple or alternate strings of events rattle the bars of the national tradition and the history manuals whose very constraints and necessities their parodic force indicts. Narrative invention here thus by way of its very implausibility becomes the figure of a larger possibility of praxis, its compensation but also its affirmation in the form of projection and mimetic reenactment" (1991, 369).

6. See, for example, Street Noises: Parisian Pleasure, 1900–40 (1993), by Adrian Rifkin, for a discussion of the popular construction of the archetypal Parisian in the early twentieth century.

7. Her end recalls the death of the British Consul in Malcolm Lowry's Under the Volcano. In this novel, what Lowry portrays as the violence of Mexico works in tandem with the Consul's propensity toward self-destruction. Murdered in a foul cantina on the outskirts of Cuernavaca, the Consul is then thrown into a nearby ravine.

8. This dissolution of boundaries rather closely recalls Roger Caillois's discussion in "Paris, mythe moderne," of the Fantómas books: "the imaginary fissure that separates the Paris of appearances from the Paris of mysteries has been filled in. The two cities that initially co-existed without mingling have now been reduced to one. At first the myth was content to use the night and the marginal areas, the unknown alleyways and the unexplored catacombs. But it quickly took over the light of day and the heart of the city. It occupies the most frequented, the most official, the most reassuring buildings. Notre Dame, the Louvre, and the Police Headquarters have become its chosen lands. Nothing escapes its contagion; everywhere the mythical has contaminated the real" (my translation, 1937, 689).

9. Lucie suggests light (enlightenment), Lucifer, and also one of the vampires in Bram Stoker's Dracula.

10. The idea of a hole underlying the center of Paris brings to mind Nadja's insistence (in André Breton's Nadja, 1960) that there is a secret tunnel connecting key points of the city, as well as Pierre Véry's Fantómas, who penetrates "the center [literally "heart"] of the earth" by means of "incredible elevators" (my translation, 1931, 178). All these underground tunnels are related to the sewers of Paris, which had exercised the imagination for some time. Both Hugo and Balzac made use of them as settings. Dean McCannell comments on the exciting "realization that all the social establishments of the city—be they domestic, commercial, industrial, or cultural—no matter how unrelated they are on the surface, are interconnected underground . . ." (75).

11. This passage was probably inspired by Fuentes's reading of El recurso del método. In an interview with Julio Ortega he comments, "There is a memorable moment in El recurso del método when the exiled dictator begins to fill his Parisian apartment with monkeys, cockatoos, vines, and hammocks; he starts turning it into San Salvador" (my translation, 1989, 642). Actually, Carpentier limits his protagonist to a hammock and tropical cuisine. The monkeys, cockatoos, and vines are Fuentes's contribution to El recurso.

12. This enigmatic incident may have been inspired by the brief references

in biographies of Dumas père to Alexis, the boy from Martinique who was given to Dumas by Marie Dorval and who thereafter formed part of the household staff (Maurois 1957, 233–234).

13. Margaret Sayers Peden develops this idea in her essay (1981).

14. For Ortega, it is one of the few novels that really succeeds in making the reader responsible for his or her interpretation of the text (1989, 647).

CHAPTER 6. NO MAN'S LAND: *REENCUENTRO DE PERSONAJES*

1. All translations of Garro's novel (1982) are my own.

2. In this interview with Michele Muncy, she explains the inception of the novel in terms of this meeting (1986, 67), but I shall argue later that she had a more pressing motive for writing.

3. Implicit in this comment, as I shall argue later, is the insistence that Octavio Paz, who has set out to do just what she describes here, is *not* that genius.

4. There is a tendency in *Tender Is the Night* as well to view the city as not quite real. It is a dreamworld, where bizarre and sometimes frightening things—like the sequence involving the murdered black man—may happen, and where the North American expatriates can cavort as they will without much fear of censure.

5. The protagonist of Jean Rhys's *Good Morning, Midnight* (1930) is exploited by the owner of a dreary Paris dress shop, where she works. A small bequest frees her from that particular prison. In their extreme dependence, Rhys's protagonists, who are victimized by their lovers as well as their precarious economic situations, are not unlike Verónica.

CHAPTER 7. PARIS IS BURNING: *PAISAJES DESPUÉS DE LA BATALLA*

1. I have used Helen Lane's translation (1987) for quotations. The page numbers of the English edition appear first, followed by those of the Spanish edition (1982) cited in the bibliography.

2. Randolph Pope argues that "the rejection of an imposed and repulsive past, a central activity in the previous novels, does not exist here; but, on the other hand, *the past does not exist* except as debris" (1990, 60). I would argue that the gesture of reducing the past—and the city—to ruins constitutes a very definite form of rejection with a large component of wishful thinking.

3. In *La Goutte d'or* (1985), Michel Tournier explores the loss of innocence of a young oasis dweller who winds up in this section of Paris. Although virtually everyone he meets is either Arab or has some stake in Arab life, he is nonetheless appropriated by the "culture of the image" (i.e., consumer society), which is, of course, alien to his native values.

4. I am using *modernity* here in John Tomlinson's sense. For Tomlinson, "the drift towards a sort of global cultural homogeneity" derives from the dominance of a "modern" way of life, whose determinants "include urbanism, mass communications, a technical-scientific-rationalist dominant ideology, a system of (mainly secular) nation-states, a particular way of organising social space

and experience and a certain subjective-existential mode of individual self-awareness" (1991, 27).

5. As an epic of modern life, *Paisajes* belongs to the class of books that Fredric Jameson describes as the "satire-collage": "the form taken by artificial epic [composed in writing, not orally] in the degraded world of commodity production and the mass media; it is artificial epic whose raw materials have become spurious and inauthentic, monumental gesture now replaced by the cultural junk of industrial capitalism" (1979, 80).

6. As early as 1931, Georges Simenon described the Marais in similar terms, but with marked disapproval: "The name of the place, displayed in ceramic letters, was Au Roi de Sicile. Below it were inscriptions in Hebrew, Polish, and other incomprehensible languages, probably including Russian. . . . Less than a hundred yards away were the Rue de Rivoli and the Rue Saint-Antoine—wide and well lit, with their buses, their shops, and their police" (*Pietr le Letton*, quoted in Rifkin 1993, 3).

7. David Mamet's comments on Disneyland are to the point here: "One creates for oneself the idea that things at Disneyland are being done for one's own good . . . [and] (with a great deal of help) the idea that Every Thing Not Required is Forbidden. And so we see, as in any other totalitarian state, the internalization of authority, and its transformation into a Sense of Right" (1989, 83).

8. See especially "Proceso a la izquierda" and "Marginalidad y disidencia: La nueva información revolucionaria" in *Libertad, libertad, libertad* (1978).

9. In "Proceso a la izquierda," he excoriates politicians right and left because "they eliminate every notion of transcendence from their vocabulary— the unsolvable mystery of the creation of material, the reality of suffering, the inevitable tragedy of old age and death . . . ," because they refuse to question "such highly questionable ideas as normality, State, property, marriage, family, [industrialization, and consumerism]" and, ultimately, because they offer "no alternative in terms of the imagination and utopia" (my translation, 1978, 78).

10. Goytisolo has taken some liberties here. On the morning before the actual funeral, Aragon's body was displayed at the offices of the French Communist Party on the Place du Colonel-Fabien. For a period of three hours, several thousand people filed by the casket to pay their last respects, according to *Le Monde* (29 December 1982, 1; 26).

11. Similar in intention is a scene that takes place in the Louvre, where, we find "bewildered polyglot groups trooping through its halls, never quite certain if the guide is going to recite the list of Merovingian kings of France to them or offer them a ride in a gondola, and dozens of Japanese examining the Mona Lisa through tinted glasses" (52; 69). However, the sweeper's translation of "Elsa" also suggests the kind of negotiation between cultures that allows the target group to retain a measure of autonomy. For a discussion of this sort of accommodation, see Tomlinson 1991, 45–47.

12. This discovery calls to mind James L. Clifford's assertion that "identity is conjunctural, not essential" (1988, 11). Clifford conceives of cultures "not as organically unified or traditionally continuous but rather as negotiated present processes" (1988, 273).

13. Balzac's description of the boarding house in *Le Père Goriot* is, of course, the subject of a chapter on the beginnings of modern realism in Auerbach's *Mimesis*. It is just possible that Goytisolo had Auerbach's book in mind when he wrote this description that ultimately subverts any sense of realism. He refers to the Sentier as "that somewhat Balzacian decor" (11, 20).

14. At another point, he refers to them as "characters straight out of an operetta, immured behind manners, a language, and memories that went back thirty years" (117; 146).

15. In the fictive Goytisolo's case, it really is the mind that is wandering, since his constitutional appears to be a strictly mental exercise. It is not clear that he ever leaves his apartment.

16. In his Swiftian essay on the New York City blackout, "Modesta proposición a los príncipes de consumo de nuestra bella sociedad de consumo" (1978, 150–56), Goytisolo describes the looters as "members of an unofficial but real association of frustrated clients who have been unjustly deprived of the right to satisfy the voracious appetite for consumption that is stimulated by all of the forms of publicity known to a system that is unable . . . to provide them with a means of satisfaction" (my translation, 153). He adds that the same situation exists in big cities throughout Western Europe.

17. This vision of the disinterested intellectual as a pariah is not so far from Karl Mannheim's description of the essential "homelessness" (by this he means detachment from a fixed social stratum) that provides the intelligentsia with a measure of ideological freedom (1936, 153–66).

18. His development of this ideal must have impressed Said, whose description of the figure that today incarnates the intellectual mission of liberation—"the migrant . . . the intellectual and artist in exile, the political figure between domains, between forms, between homes, and between languages"—accords closely with Goytisolo's ideas (Said 1993, 332).

19. After the hecatomb, the protagonist is "dismembered torn to bits like your own story" (156; 192). For a discussion of the relation between the narrative voices in the text and the fragmented protagonist, see Blasco 1985.

Bibliography

Aldao, Martín. 1943. *La vida falsa*. Buenos Aires: Imprenta Belmonte.

Appiah, Kwame Anthony. 1995. The Postcolonial and the Postmodern. *The Post-colonial Studies Reader*. Eds. Bill Ashcroft, Gareth Griffiths, and Helen Tiffin. London and New York: Routledge. 119–25.

Après la mort de Louis Aragon. 1982. *Le Monde* (Paris), 26–27 December, 6.

Aragon, Louis. 1970. *Nightwalker (Le Paysan de Paris)*. Trans. and afterword by Frederic Brown. Englewood Cliffs, N.J.: Prentice-Hall.

Bakhtin, M. M. 1981. *The Dialogic Imagination*. Ed. Michael Holquist. Trans. Caryl Emerson and Michael Holquist. Austin: University of Texas Press.

Balderston, Daniel. 1983. Review of *Testimonios sobre Mariana*, by Elena Garro. *Hispámerica* 36: 114–16.

Baudelaire, Charles. 1958. Le Cygne. *Flowers of Evil: A Selection*. Ed. Marthiel Mathews and Jackson Mathews. New York: New Directions. 78–83.

Benjamin, Walter. 1978. Surrealism. *Reflections*. Trans. Edmund Jephcott. New York: Harcourt Brace Jovanovich. 177–85.

Benstock, Shari. 1986. *Women of the Left Bank: Paris, 1900–1940*. Austin: University of Texas Press.

Bianco, José. 1978. *La pérdida del reino*. Caracas: Monte Avila.

Blasco, Javier Francisco. 1985. El palimsesto urbano de "Paisajes después de la batalla." *Anales de la literatura española contemporánea* 10, nos. 1–3:11–29.

Blest Gana, Alberto. 1936. *Los transplantados*. Santiago, Chile: Nascimento.

Boldy, Steven. 1980. *The Novels of Julio Cortázar*. Cambridge: Cambridge University Press.

Borges, Jorge Luis. 1980. El arte narrativo y la magia. *Prosa completa*. 2 vols. Barcelona: Bruguera. Vol 1. 163–70.

Breton, André. 1960. *Nadja*. Trans. Richard Howard. New York: Grove Press.

Buck-Morss, Susan. 1989. *The Dialectics of Seeing: Walter Benjamin and the Arcades Project*. Cambridge: MIT Press.

Buñuel, Luis. 1992. *Mi último suspiro*. 3rd ed. Trans. Ana María de la Fuente. Barcelona: Plaza y Janés.

Butor, Michel. 1985. La ville comme texte. *L'art des confins*. Ed. Annie Cazenave and Jean-François Lyotard. Paris: Presses Universitaires de France. 71–78.

Caillois, Roger. 1937. Paris, mythe moderne. *Nouvelle Revue Française* 48:682–99.

Cambaceres, Eugenio. 1956. Música sentimental. *Obras completas*. Ed. E. M. S. Danero. Sante Fe, Argentina: Castellví. 93–151.

Campbell, Joseph. 1949. *The Hero with a Thousand Faces*. New York: Pantheon.

Campos, Haroldo de. 1980. Beyond Exclusive Languages. *Latin America in Its Literature.* Eds. César Fernández Moreno, Julio Ortega, and Ivan A. Schulman. Trans. Mary G. Berg. New York: Holmes and Meier. 221–43.

Cardinal, Roger. 1986. *Breton: Nadja.* London: Grant and Cutler.

Carpentier, Alejo. 1976. *Reasons of State.* Trans. Frances Partridge. New York: Alfred A. Knopf.

———. 1974. Interview. By Miguel F. Roa. *El Día* (Mexico), 19 June, 16.

———. 1974a. *El recurso del método.* Mexico: Siglo Veintiuno.

———. 1964. Problemática de la actual novela latinoamericana. *Tientos y diferencias.* Mexico: Universidad Nacional Autónoma de Mexico. 7–31.

Carroll, David. 1987. Narrative, Heterogeneity, and the Question of the Political: Bakhtin and Lyotard. *The Aims of Representation.* Ed. Murray Krieger. New York: Columbia University Press. 162–183.

Casal, Julián del. 1963 Ultima ilusión. *Prosas.* 3 vols. Havana: Consejo Nacional de Cultura. Vol. 1. 226–29.

Clifford, James L. 1992. Traveling Cultures. *Cultural Studies.* Eds. Lawrence Grossberg, Cary Nelson, and Paula Treichler. New York: Routledge. 96–116.

———. 1988. *The Predicament of Culture: Twentieth-Century Ethnography, Literature, and Art.* Cambridge: Harvard University Press.

Collier, Peter. 1985. Surrealist City Narrative: Breton and Aragon. *Unreal City: Urban Experience in Modern European Literature and Art.* Ed. Edward Timms. Manchester: Manchester University Press. 214–28.

Cortázar, Julio. 1987. *Rayuela.* Barcelona: Edhasa.

———. 1985. *La fascinación de las palabras: Conversaciones con Julio Cortázar.* Interviews by Omar Prego. Barcelona: Muchnik.

———. 1983. Interview. By Karl Kohut. *Escribir en París.* Frankfurt: Vervuert. 197–222.

———. 1966. *Hopscotch.* Trans. Gregory Rabassa. New York: Random House.

Coulson, Graciela. 1974. Los cuentos de Ribeyro: Primer Encuentro. *Cuadernos Americanos* 95, no. 4 (July-August): 220–226.

Culler, Jonathan. 1982. Semiotics of Tourism. *American Journal of Semiotics* 1, nos. 1–2: 127–140.

Darío, Rubén. 1950–1955. Autobiografía. *Obras completas.* 8 vols. Madrid: Afrodisio Aguado. Vol. 1. 15–177.

Debord, Guy. 1977. *Society of the Spectacle.* Detroit: Black and Red.

Descartes, René. 1925. *Discours de la méthode.* Paris: J. Vrin.

Díaz Rodríguez, Manuel. 1919. *Idolos rotos.* Madrid: América.

———. N.d. *Sangre patricia.* Madrid: Sociedad española de librería.

Dictionnaire critique et documentaire des peintres, sculpteurs, dessinateurs et graveurs. 1948–1955. Ed. E. Bénézit. 8 vols. Paris: Librairie Gründ.

Dohmann, Barbara, and Luis Harss. 1966. *Los nuestros.* Buenos Aires: Sudamericana.

Dorfman, Ariel. 1982. Entre Proust y la momia americana: siete notas y un epílogo sobre "El recurso del método." *Revista Iberoamericana* 114–15: 95–128.

During, Simon. 1995. Postmodernism or Post-colonialism Today. *The Post-*

colonial Studies Reader. Eds. Bill Ashcroft, Gareth Griffiths, and Helen Tiffin. London and New York: Routledge. 125–29.

Edwards Bello, Joaquín. 1933. *Criollos en París*. Santiago, Chile: Nascimento.

Evenson, Norma. 1979. *Paris: A Century of Change, 1878–1978*. New Haven and London: Yale University Press.

Fanon, Frantz. 1968. *The Wretched of the Earth*. Trans. Constance Farrington. New York: Grove Press.

Faris, Wendy B. 1983. *Carlos Fuentes*. New York: Ungar.

———. 1980. Alejo Carpentier à la recherche du temps perdu. *Comparative Literature Studies* 17:133–54.

Fitzgerald, F. Scott. 1951. *Tender Is the Night*. New York: Scribner.

Flaubert, Gustave. 1986. *Bouvard et Pécuchet*. Paris: Flammarion.

———. 1984. *L'Education sentimentale: Histoire d'un jeune homme*. Paris: Garnier.

Fleurs latines des dames et des gens du monde. N.d. Ed. P. Larousse. Paris: Veuve P. Larrouse.

Franco, Jean. 1976. París, ciudad fabulosa. *Novelistas hispanoamericanos de hoy*. Ed. Juan Loveluck. Madrid: Taurus. 271–290.

Frye, Northrop. 1976. *The Secular Scripture: A Study of the Structure of Romance*. Cambridge: Harvard University Press.

———. 1965. Varieties of Literary Utopias. *Daedalus* (Spring): 323–47.

———. 1957. *The Anatomy of Criticism*. Princeton, N.J.: Princeton University Press.

Fuentes, Carlos. 1989. Carlos Fuentes: Para recuperar la tradición de la Mancha. Interview by Julio Ortega. *Revista Iberoamericana* 55:637–54.

———. 1988. La tradición literaria latinoamericana. *La obra de Carlos Fuentes: Una visión múltiple*. Ed. Ana María Hernández de López. Madrid: Pliegos. 19–27.

———. 1982. *Distant Relations*. Trans. Margaret Sayers Peden. New York: Farrar, Straus and Giroux.

———. 1980. Entrevista a Carlos Fuentes. By Saul Sosnowski. *Hispamérica* 9, no. 27 (December): 69–97.

———. 1980a. *Una familia lejana*. Mexico: Ediciones Era.

———. 1975. *Terra nostra*. Mexico: Joaquín Mortíz.

———. 1970. Luis Buñuel: El cine como libertad. *Casa con dos puertas*. Mexico: Joaquín Mortiz. 197–215.

———. 1969. *La nueva novela hispanoamericana*. Mexico. Joaquín Mortiz.

Fussell, Paul. 1980. *Abroad: British Literary Traveling Between the Wars*. Oxford and New York: Oxford University Press.

García Gabaldón, Jesús. 1988. El futuro ya existe. *Químera* 73 (January): 51–54.

García Márquez, Gabriel. El rastro de tu sangre en la nieve. *Doce cuentos peregrinos*. Bogotá: La Oveja Negra, 1992. 199–226.

Garro, Elena. 1992. *Memorias de España 1937*. Mexico and Madrid: Siglo Veintiuno.

———. 1986. Encuentro con Elena Garro. Interview by Michele Muncy. *Hispanic Journal* 7.2:65–71.

————. 1982. *Reencuentro de personajes*. Mexico: Grijalba.

————. 1981. *Testimonios sobre Mariana*. Grijalbo.

————. 1978. Entrevista con Elena Garro. By Joseph Sommers. *26 autoras del México actual*. Eds. Beth Miller and Alfonso González. Mexico: Costa-Amica. 204–19.

————. 1979. A mí se me ha ocurrido todo al revés. *Cuadernos Hispánicos* 346:38–51.

Gombrich, E. H. 1960. *Art and Illusion: A Study of the Psychology of Pictorial Representation*. New York: Pantheon.

Gómez Carrillo, Enrique. 1974. *Treinta años de mi vida*. Guatemala: José de Pineda Ibarra.

————. 1906. *Maravillas: Novela funambulesca*. Paris: La Viuda de Charles Bouret.

González Echevarría, Roberto. 1985. *Alejo Carpentier: The Pilgrim at Home*. Ithaca, N.Y.: Cornell University Press.

————. 1977. *The Voice of the Masters: Writing and Authority in Modern Latin American Literature*. Austin: University of Texas Press.

Goytisolo, Juan. 1988. Regreso al origen. Interview by Miguel Riera. *Química* 73 (January): 36–40.

————. 1987. *Landscapes After the Battle*. Trans. Helen Lane. New York: Seaver Books, 1987.

————. 1985. La libertad de los parias: Interview by Randolph Pope. *Espejo de escritores*. Hanover, N.H.: Ediciones del Norte. 105–128.

————. 1984. Interview by Julio Ortega. Trans. Joseph Schraibman. *The Review of Contemporary Fiction* 4, no. 2:4–19.

————. 1982. *Paisajes después de la batalla*. Barcelona: Contemporáneos.

————. 1978. *Libertad, libertad, libertad*. Barcelona: Anagrama.

————. 1975. Cronología. *Juan Goytisolo*. Ed. Gonzalo Sobejano. Madrid: Espiral. 5–22.

Groussac, Paul. 1884. *Fruto vedado: Costumbres argentinas*. Buenos Aires: M. Biedma.

Güiraldes, Ricardo. 1932. *Raucho, momentos de una juventud contemporánea*. Madrid: Espasa Calpe.

Gutiérrez Nájera, Manuel. 1958. Stora y las medias parisienses. *Cuentos completos y otras narraciones*. Ed. E. K. Mapes. Mexico: Fondo de Cultura Económica. 81–84.

Gyurko, Lanin A. 1983. Identity and the Double in Fuentes's "Una familia lejana." *Ibero-Amerikanisches Archiv*. Neue Folge 9, no. 1:15–58.

Hemingway, Ernest. 1954. *The Sun Also Rises*. New York: Charles Scribner's Sons.

Hollier, Denis. 1989. *Against Architecture: The Writings of Georges Bataille*. Trans. Betsy Wing. Cambridge: MIT Press.

Holst Petersen, Kirsten, and Anna Rutherford, eds. 1996. *A Double Colonization: Colonial and Post-Colonial Women's Writing*. Mundelstop, Australia: Dangaroo Press.

Howe, Irving. 1971. The City in Literature. *Commentary* 51 (May): 61–65.

Hugo, Victor. 1965. *The Hunchback of Notre Dame.* Trans. Walter J. Cobb. New York: New American Library.

———. 1855. *Poésies.* 2 vols. Paris: L. Hachette.

———. 1985. *A Theory of Parody.* New York: Methuen.

Hutcheon, Linda. 1995. Circling the Downspout of Empire. *The Post-colonial Studies Reader.* Eds. Bill Ashcroft, Gareth Griffiths, and Helen Tiffin. London and New York: Routledge. 130–36.

———. 1989. *The Politics of Postmodernism.* New York: Routledge.

Jameson, Frederic. 1991. *Postmodernism, or The Cultural Logic of Late Capitalism.* Durham, N.C.: Duke University Press.

———. 1986. Third-World Literature in the Era of Multinational Capitalism. *Social Text* 15 (Fall): 65–88.

———. 1984. Periodizing the '60s. *The Sixties without Apology.* Eds. Sohnya Sayres, Anders Stephanson, Stanley Aronowitz, and Frederic Jameson. Minneapolis: University of Minnesota Press. 175–83.

———. 1979. *Fables of Aggression: Wyndham Lewis, the Modernist as Fascist.* Berkeley and Los Angeles: University of California Press.

———. 1975. Magical Narratives: Romance as Genre. *New Literary History* 7:135–64.

Kadir, Djelal. 1986. *Questing Fictions: Latin America's Family Romance.* Minneapolis: University of Minneapolis Press.

Kaplan, Marina. 1994. The Latin American Romance in Sarmiento, Borges, Ribeyro, Cortázar, and Rulfo. *Sarmiento: Author of a Nation.* Eds. Tulio Halperín Donghi and Iván Jaksic. Berkeley and Los Angeles: University of California Press. 314–46.

Kennedy, J. Gerald. 1993. *Imagining Paris: Exile, Writing, and American Identity.* New Haven: Yale University Press.

Kohut, Karl. 1983. Introducción. *Escribir en París: Entrevistas con Fernando Arrabal, Adelaïda Blásquez, José Corrales Egea, Julio Cortázar. Agustín Gómera Arcos, Juan Goytisolo, Augusto Roa Bastos, Severo Sarduy y Jorge Semprún.* Ed. Karl Kohut. Frankfurt: Verlag Klaus Dieter Vervuert. 11–35.

Kramer, Lloyd S. 1988. *Threshold of a New World: Intellectuals and the Exile Experience in Paris, 1830–1848.* Ithaca and London: Cornell University Press.

Krysinski, Wodzimerz. 1987. *Carrefours de signes: Essais sur le roman moderne.* La Haye: Mouton Editeur.

Leed, Eric J. 1991. *The Mind of the Traveler: From Gilgamesh to Global Tourism.* New York: Basic Books.

López, Lucio V. 1915. Don Polidoro (Retrato de muchos). *Recuerdos de viaje.* Buenos Aires: La Cultura Argentina. 349–61.

Luchting, Wolfgang. 1983. Los mecanismos de la ambigüedad: "La juventud en la otra ribera" de Julio Ramón Ribeyro. *Iberomanía* 17:131–50.

———. 1975. Un Henry James peruano? *Chasqui* 4, no. 3 (May): 64–67.

Mâle, Emile. 1958. *The Gothic Image: Religious Art in France in the Thirteenth Century.* Trans. Dora Nussey. New York: Harper.

Mallea, Eduardo. 1945. *La bahia de silencio.* Buenos Aires: Sudamericana.

Mamet, David. 1989. A Party for Mickey Mouse. *Some Freaks*. New York: Viking. 78–84.

Mannheim, Karl. 1936. *Ideology and Utopia*. Trans. Louis Wirth and Edward Shils. New York: Harcourt, Brace and World.

Manuel, Frank E. 1965. Toward a Psychological History of Utopias. *Daedalus* 94 (Spring): 293–323.

Maurois, André. 1957. *Three Musketeers*. Trans. Gerard Hopkins. London: Jonathan Cape.

McCannell, Dean. 1976. *The Tourist: A New Theory of the Leisure Class*. New York: Schocken Books.

McLuhan, Marshall, 1967. *The Mechanical Bride: Folklore of Industrial Man*. Boston: Beacon Press.

Molloy, Sylvia. 1972. *La Diffusion de la littérature hispano-americaine en France au XXe siècle*. Paris: Presses Unviersitaires de France.

Mumford, Lewis. 1970. *The Culture of Cities*. New York: Harcourt Brace Jovanovich.

Murger, Henri. 1930. *Latin Quarter*. Trans. Elizabeth Ward Hughs. Westport, Ct.: Hyperion.

Ortega, Julio. 1985. Los cuentos de Ribeyro. *Cuadernos Hispanoamericanos* 417 (March): 128–45.

Oud-Dine Bammamu, Nadjm. 1977. Space in Islam. Trans. Anthony F. Roberts. *Cultures* 5, no. 4:42–57.

Panofsky, Erwin. 1957. *Gothic Architecture and Scholasticism*. New York: Meridian Books.

Paz, Octavio. 1959. *El laberinto de la soledad*. Mexico: Fondo de Cultura Económica.

Peden, Margaret Sayers. 1981. Forking Paths, Infinite Novels, Ultimate Narrators. *Carlos Fuentes: A Critical View*. Eds. Robert Brody and Charles Rossman. Austin: University of Texas Press. 156–72.

Pérez Galdás, Benito. 1971. *Lo prohibido*. Madrid: Castalia.

Piehler, H. A. 1953. *Paris for Everyman*. London: J. M. Dent and Sons.

Piehler, Paul. 1971. *The Visionary Landscape: A Study in Medieval Allegory*. London: Edward Arnold.

Pike, Burton. 1981. *The Image of the City in Modern Literature*. Princeton, N.J.: Princeton University Press.

Pope, Randolph. 1990. Writing after the Battle: Juan Goytisolo's Renewal. *Literature, the Arts, and Democracy: Spain in the Eighties*. Ed. Samuel Amell. London: Associated University Presses. 58–66.

Prendergast, Christopher. 1991. Framing the City: Two Parisian Windows. *City Images: Perspectives from Literature, Philosophy, and Film*. Ed. Mary Ann Caws. New York: Gordon and Breach.

Presentación. 1966. *Mundo Nuevo* 1 (July): 4.

Proust, Marcel. 1934. *Remembrance of Things Past*. Trans. C. K. Scott Moncrieff. 2 vols. New York: Random House.

Queneau, Raymond. 1959. *Zazie dans le métro*. Paris: Gallimard.

Rama, Angel. Prólogo. 1977. *Poesía*. By Rubén Darío. Caracas: Ayacucho. 9–52.

———. 1976. *Los dictadores latinoamericanos*. Mexico: Fondo de Cultura Económica.

Reiss, Timothy J. 1982. Power, Poetry, and the Resemblance of Nature. *Mimesis: From Mirror to Method*. Eds. and intro. John D. Lyons and Stephen G. Nichols Jr. Hanover, N.H.: University Presses of New England.

Ribeyro, Julio Ramón. 1983. La juventud en la otra ribera. *La juventud en la otra ribera*. Lima: Argos Vergara. 274–309.

———. 1977. El encanto de la burguesía es discreto. *Escritores peruanos que piensan que dicen*. Ed. Wolfgang Luchting. Lima: Ecoma. 43–61.

Rifkin, Adrian. 1993. *Street Noises: Parisian Pleasure, 1900–40*. Manchester: Manchester University Press.

Romero, José Luis. 1976. *Latinoamérica: Las ciudades y las ideas*. Mexico City: Siglo Veintiuno.

Rudorff, Raymond. 1972. *The Belle Epoque: Paris in the Nineties*. New York: Saturday Review Press.

Saalman, Howard. 1971. *Haussmann: Paris Transformed*. New York: George Braziller.

Said, Edward W. 1993. *Culture and Imperialism*. New York: Alfred A. Knopf.

Salazar Bondy, Sebastián. 1958. *Pobre gente de París*. Lima: Juan Mejía Baca.

Salinas, Pedro. 1968. *La poesía de Rubén Darío*. Buenos Aires: Losada.

Sarmiento, Domingo F. 1981. *Viajes*. Buenos Aires: Editorial de Belgrano.

Savigneau, Josyane. 1982. La mémoire naissante. *Le Monde* (Paris), 29 December: 26.

Seigel, Jerrold E. 1986. *Bohemian Paris: Culture, Politics and the Boundaries of Bourgeois Life, 1830–1932*. New York: Viking.

Solar, Alberto del. 1890. *Rastaquouère: Ilusiones y desengaños sudamericanos en París*. Buenos Aires: F. Lajouane.

Stein, Gertrude. 1973. *Everybody's Autobiography*. New York: Vintage Books.

Stevens, John. 1973. *Medieval Romance: Themes and Approaches*. London: Hutchinson.

Starkie, Enid. 1954. *Petrus Borel: The Lycanthrope*. London: Faber and Faber.

Terdiman, Richard. 1985. Deconstructing Memory: On Representing the Past and Theorizing Culture in France Since the Revolution. *Diacritics* 15.4 (Winter): 13–37.

Tomlinson, John. 1991. *Cultural Imperialism: A Critical Introduction*. Baltimore: Johns Hopkins University Press.

Tournier, Michel. 1985. *La Goutte d'or*. Paris: Gallimard.

Véry, Pierre. 1931. *Les Métamorphoses*. Paris: Nouvelle Revue Français.

Viñas, David. 1964. *Literatura argentina y realidad política*. Buenos Aires: J. Alvárez.

Waugh, Evelyn. 1945. *Brideshead Revisited*. Boston: Little, Brown.

———. *The Diaries of Evelyn Waugh*. Ed. Michael Davie. Boston: Little, Brown.

White, Hayden. 1973. *Metahistory: the Historical Imagination in Nineteenth-Century Europe*. Baltimore: Johns Hopkins University Press.

Wyers Weber, Frances. 1983. Los contextos de Carpentier. *Revista Iberoamericana* 123–24: 323–34.

Index